"TWO-GETHER INTIMATELY"....

♥ "This author is real – down to earth. It is nice to know someone else has had the same frustrations and inhibitions! I'm not alone! I really appreciated Ruth's honesty, frankness and transparency – I can relate to her!"

♥ "I loved the humorous and light approach to this delicate topic. It was not a starchy sermon! I began reading this book with my defenses up and finished feeling enriched, encouraged and excited!"

♥ "As an engaged woman, I feel I have really gotten a head-start on this area of my marital relationship."

♥ "I learned more about how to deal with my painful past by reading this book than in eight years of counselling."

♥ "This book is Biblically sound, theologically correct, and a great resource for premarital counselling." (Theology professor)

♥ "A positive, practical and constructive book – very useful as a counselling resource." (Chartered Psychologist)

♥ "Where was this book forty years ago? Finally, someone has addressed this traditionally taboo topic in a very tasteful, yet frank manner. I'm so glad I read it; you are never too old to improve! A book every women should read."

♥ "An easy-reading book, well organized with a methodical approach. I really appreciated the questions for reflection at the end of each chapter."

♥ "I plan to reread this book on a yearly basis, as it helped create renewed excitement and passion for my mate. A marital enrichment resource I will keep."

♥ "The information given in this book enlightened me to many aspects of intimacy that I was previously unaware of. I will be a better wife and lover as a result. My attitude and thoughts have changed toward my husband's needs and my desire to meet them."

♥ "Being a busy mother of two preschoolers, I really needed help in improving this aspect of our marriage. I appreciated the fact that Ruth was ordinary, not a professional sex specialist. She inspired me!"

Two-gether Intimately...

Understanding & Meeting Your Husband's Sexual Needs

Ruth D. Clarence

Sixth Edition

Two-gether™
Publishing

Two-gether Intimately...

Understanding & Meeting
Your Husband's Sexual Needs

Published by Two-gether™ Publishing
1348 Oakland Cres.
Devon, Alberta, Canada T9G 2E5
www.intimacyseminar.com

Scripture quotations marked (NIV) are taken from the Holy Bible, New International Version ® NIV ®, Copyright © 1973, 1978, 1984 by International Bible Society. Used by permission of Zondervan Publishing House. All rights reserved.

Scripture quotations marked (TLB) are taken from The Living Bible, Copyright © 1971. Used by permission of Tyndale House Publishers Inc., Wheaton, Illinois 60189. All rights reserved.

Scripture quotations marked (KJV) are taken from the King James Version.

Two-gether™ Publishing has made every effort to trace ownership of all quotes and ideas in this book. In the event of a question arising from the use of a quote, we regret any error made and will be pleased to make the necessary correction in future editions of this book.

The author does not necessarily endorse the entire contents of all publications referred to in this book.

Photos within by Glamor Magic.

ISBN 0-9686613-2-7

Printed in Canada

Table Of Contents

Part One: **UNDERSTANDIN**

Chapter 1
How God Views Sex...........................

Chapter 2
How Your Past
Affects Your Present Sexual Life.........

Chapter 3
How Men Are Wired..........................

Chapter 4
How the Seasons of Your Marriage
Affect Your Sexual Life ....

Chapter 5
How Men Feel....................................

Part Two: **MEETING**

Chapter 6
How to Discuss Your Sexual
Relationship With Your Mate..............

Chapter 7
How to Plan Your Sex Life ....

Chapter 8
How to Make Romance
A Part of Every Day ....

Conclusion ....

Appendix ....

Dedication

*T*his book is dedicated
with deepest love and affection
to my dear husband
Simon Sinclair.

*H*is love, encouragement,
wisdom, and patience
have inspired me to be the best I can be
and to share what we have learned
Two-gether.

Ecclesiastes 4:9 & 12

Acknowledgements

First – to God, the Wise and All Powerful Creator, who lovingly designed us with the ability to enjoy the delights of marital sexual intimacy, and who gave us His Word to instruct us how.

Special thanks:

To Simon, my husband – You have supported me in *every* way possible during this project. Thank you for allowing me to share our story.

To Jenna and James, our children - My "womb-mates." You are the *best* gifts Daddy and I have ever received! Thanks for your support of Mommy's project.

To Mrs. Doris Rome, my mother – Thanks for all of your research assistance, endless encouragement, and concerted prayer support. You have always been the "wind beneath my wings" and a real model of excellence.

To Dr. Paul Rome, my brother – Your evaluation and critique of this work have been outstanding and invaluable. Thanks for all your encouragement to believe in myself and to expand my horizons. Thanks also for providing many research resources to assist in this project.

To Hilda Siggelkow, Alberta District Women's Ministries Director, for providing the first opportunity for me to share this information at the Provincial Women's Retreat. Thanks for taking the risk!

Also, thanks to: Dr. Gordon Franklin, Dr. Larry Froese, Dr. George Feller, Mrs. Moira Feller, Rev. William Olson, Rev. Rosswell Olson, Mrs. Doris Rome, Mrs. Robina Baker, Mrs. Alanna Gronberg, Mrs. Hilda Siggelkow, Mrs. Daisy Keys, and Mr. Gordon White for your excellent editorial assistance. Also to Tom and Ilene Cook.

Thanks to the many men and women who responded to my various questionnaires. Your input was so appreciated.

Typeset and Design: Mrs. Dawn Rouncville – You are the best! Your artistic flair, diligence to detail, and impeccable typesetting expertise have made this a very attractive book!

Logo Creation and Design: Mrs. Doris Rome.

Proofreaders: Mrs. Cheryl Chiesa – Thanks for all of your encouragement to pursue these new ventures, and for all your help in achieving them. Also thanks to Georgina Baxter and Christine Lyseng Savage.

Prayer Team: Mrs. Doris Rome, Mr. Ken Rome, Mrs. Louise Goodbrand, Mrs. Val Bray, and Mrs. Cheryl Chiesa. The strength of your prayers has been felt throughout this entire project. Many thanks!

General Editor: Dr. K. Paul Rome

ntroduction

A Word From the Other Side of the Bed

Approximately five years ago, after concluding a pastoral counselling session, I asked Ruth, my wife, if she would consider speaking with the ladies of our church on the topic of "Understanding and Meeting Your Husband's Sexual Needs."

In previous months, I had encountered several couples who sought more information on the sexual aspects of marriage. Due to the delicate nature of a couple's sexual relations, it was not a topic that could be dealt with adequately in a public, family-oriented church service.

It was obvious that, as a male pastor, I could not fully understand a woman's perspective or some of the struggles that women experience. Hence, a woman-to-woman dialogue had the potential to be much more effective.

Ruth responded to my question by stating that she did not have any reservations about discussing sexual issues, provided it was done in a tasteful, Christian context. However, she voiced two concerns.

First, she was apprehensive that if she were to conduct a workshop on this topic, it might somehow give people in our church the impression that we had "perfected" this area of our marriage. While we had a healthy and growing marital relationship, she certainly didn't want to give the inaccurate impression that we were "sex-perts".

Secondly, she felt that it would be impossible to share on such a topic without some references to our own sexual life, and she questioned whether we would want to share this private information with our congregation.

After a great deal of discussion, Ruth agreed to share at our Women's Ministries meeting. She subsequently went to the Bible Bookstore and the Bible School library to do some extensive research in preparation for her talk.

Some time later, while Ruth was preparing for her presentation, she received a phone call from the Regional Women's Ministries director, who asked if she would consider speaking on the topic of "Understanding and Meeting Your Husband's Sexual Needs" at the provincial women's retreat.

Ruth was stunned at this request. She replied with laughter, "I am not always reading books on sex, but that is *exactly* the topic that I am researching for our *own* Women's Ministries meeting."

The director then exclaimed, "Well this is a confirmation! *You* are the one who should speak on this topic at this upcoming gathering!"

Ruth responded with an emphatic, "No way!" She felt that she was not qualified to address such a topic since she lacked training as a licensed sex therapist. The director strongly encouraged her to give prayerful consideration to her possible involvement.

Ruth decided to do a "test run" with our own women's group to ascertain their response.

When I announced that the subject for the next local women's meeting would be "Understanding and Meeting Your Husband's Sexual Needs," there was a very enthusiastic response, especially from the men in our congregation. Some of the men offered to take the morning off work to ensure that their wives could attend. Others confirmed that their wives would be attending, equipped with reams of paper to take copious notes.

Because of the great interest from the men and women alike, we had a record attendance at the ladies' meeting and the general response to Ruth's talk was overwhelmingly positive.

For weeks following the talk, Ruth met on a one-to-one basis with women who had posed questions and shared comments regarding this area of their marriage. This prompted Ruth to actively continue her research on the subject. She was subsequently able to act as a resource person, referring the women to many excellent books in the subject area.

After a great deal of prayer, and with the encouragement of our own church ladies, Ruth (with fear and trembling) agreed to do the workshop at the provincial retreat. She requested that another workshop be offered concurrently for those women who were not interested in or comfortable with discussing sexual issues.

Ruth worked diligently on preparing a verbatim script which I carefully reviewed and evaluated at her request.

To her surprise, approximately 350 of the 400 ladies at the retreat were in her workshop. The responses on the evaluation forms were extremely positive! The younger ladies were delighted with the presentation, and surprisingly, some of the older ladies expressed the same sentiments. "Finally, someone is talking about this much-needed topic from a tasteful, practical, and Christian perspective," one woman commented.

Other comments shared at this event included statements such as the following:

"I didn't receive any premarital counselling on this subject, and this has been an area of frustration in my marriage for years."

"Thanks for giving me so many ideas to help me initiate romance and physical intimacy in our home."

"You've released me from the guilt I've always felt about pursuing our sexual relationship."

"Thanks for talking about this important topic in a light and humorous manner."

Following the retreat, Ruth received many invitations to speak at other retreats, ladies' meetings, and banquets. We agreed that one-day workshops would be the preferred method to reach the maximum number of people with minimal stress on our family life. I jokingly teased Ruth one day by saying, "Well dear, it appears that *'Dr. Ruth Ministries'* has begun!"

Be assured that I fully support Ruth in this exciting new ministry. I believe that the Lord has opened this opportunity for service. Ruth is to be applauded for her courage in being so vulnerable and open by sharing both the things that she has done well and the things she would have done differently.

Ruth always shares very frankly and openly with her audiences that she is not:

- a nurse,
- a medical doctor,
- a sex therapist,
- or a psychologist

However, she is a woman who:

- loves the Lord with all of her heart and is a student of the Scriptures,
- loves me, her husband, intensely, and
- knew little about this aspect of marriage when we were wed, but has been willing to learn how to be an effective lover.

Ruth is *not* trying to pretend to be something she is not, but because she is sharing from a non-professional, everyday Christian woman's perspective, she has connected with the hearts of many ladies. Women have related to her frustrations and inhibitions and subsequently have been inspired to become better lovers.

My wife, over the past seventeen years of our marriage, has worked diligently at endeavoring to understand me and all of my needs. I can say without reservation that she practices what she preaches!

Enjoy this humorous, practical, and informative book. It is our prayer that your lives will be enriched and enhanced by our decision to selectively share our experiences and Biblical counsel.

(Rev.) Simon Clarence

(The other half of Two-gether™ Ministries)

Before You Begin

Our minds are like computers.
From the moment we are born, data is
entered into that internal computer
– our mind.

If quality, accurate, wholesome Biblical data is entered frequently and continuously, then the consequence will be balanced, Biblical, healthy output or behavior.

Healthy Input → **Healthy Output**

This fact is especially true as it applies to sexual information. If we have had positive, Biblical, balanced information shared and modeled for us, then we will have fewer inhibitions, less frustration and we will exhibit and develop healthy sexual responses.

In sharing with many women on this subject, I have discovered that a large percentage of them have received negative, conflicting, poor quality, or inaccurate information regarding sexuality.

Let's examine a few examples:

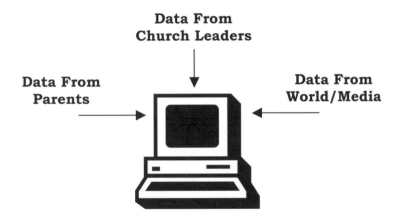

"Data" from our parents:

"Get your hands off your genitals! That's dirty!" *(from parents)*

"Suffer through sex, honey. It's your necessary duty!" *(from a mom)*

"You are my sex toy! I can do whatever I want with your body." *(from an abusive father)*

"All your father ever wants is sex, sex, sex. I get no affection in return!" *(from a mom)*

"You are ugly and stupid. No one will ever want to make love to you." *(from a father)*

"Sex is something that we just don't talk about around here." *(from parents)*

"Give your husband *his* sex – so you can have *your* children." *(from a mom)*

"Data" from SOME church or religious individuals:

"Intercourse is never without sin, but God excuses it by His grace because the estate of marriage is His work." *(Martin Luther)*

"Don't ever expect to enjoy or find sex pleasurable – that's giving in to your carnal nature!"

"If you were *really* spiritual, you wouldn't have any sexual desires. You would die to sin."

"God is disappointed in your behavior! He's angry at you for even thinking about sex."

"Sex is a result of the fall."

"Data" from the World/Media:

"Have sex with anyone, anytime! If it feels good, do it!"

"*All* women are passionate lovers and are instantly ready for sex."

"You *have* to give your boyfriend regular sex in order to keep him."

"Sexual fidelity is a thing of the past. Be liberated, baby!"

"You've got to have a gorgeous, perfect body in order to be sexy."

Does any of this data sound familiar? Input of this kind has greatly influenced the way many ladies have viewed their sexuality. With so many conflicting messages and negative voices, and in the absence of accurate Biblical information, many Christian women feel confused and bewildered.

So what are we supposed to do?

First, recognize that our genitals are *not* our most important sex organs. No, our *brains* are. The mind is the control center or hard drive (storehouse) for every sexual thought we have ever had.

This small organ weighs just over three pounds, but it has 12 billion cells and 120 trillion connections. If the mind were a computer, it would be the size of the Empire State Building.[1] Innumerable thoughts go through our computer (mind) in just one day. These thoughts determine everything about us; who we are, what we feel, and what we do.

Because this is fact, we must *choose to control* our thoughts! We must concur with Proverbs 23:7: "*We are what we think!*" (my paraphrase).

As Linda Dillon and Lorraine Pintus state in their excellent book, *Intimate Issues,*

"Most of us are better about controlling our bodies than we are about controlling our minds. We allow the ten thousand thoughts a day to trample unrestrained through our heads. Like disobedient children, they race this way and that, generating chaos and a myriad of emotions. This ought not to be, God says. He gave us our minds with the expectation that we were to rule them. He wants us to make our minds mind. God wants us, like a mother wagging her finger at a disobedient child, to tell our thoughts where they can and cannot go. God desires us to nourish certain thoughts and rebuke others saying, 'NO! I will NOT go in this direction.'"[2]

The familiar adage is true:
"*CHANGE YOUR THOUGHTS – CHANGE YOUR LIFE!*"
This is the premise and basis of this book.

It may be time for you to:

1. **ENTER** - Biblically-based, wholesome, accurate data. Create new files. Philippians 4:8 says, *"Whatever is true, whatever is noble, whatever is right, whatever is pure, whatever is lovely ... Think about such things."* (NIV).

2. **EDIT** - past thought patterns. Modify, augment or reformat old files. Ephesians 5:3-4 states, *"Let there be no sex sin among you. Dirty stories, foul talk and coarse jokes – these are not for you."* (TLB).

3. **HIGHLIGHT (BOLD)** – Reaffirm and reflect on the excellent, accurate data you have already saved and stored. Psalm 119:15 says, *"I meditate on your precepts and consider your ways."* (NIV).

4. **DELETE** - negative, ungodly, untrue data about sexuality. Proverbs 20:27 states, *"Stop listening to teaching that contradicts what you know is right."* (TLB).

We must take *personal* responsibility for our actions. We cannot continue to blame past experiences or incorrect messages from parents, the church, or media for our present sexual thoughts. We need to *choose* to make the necessary adjustments. As Colossians 3:2 says, *"Set your minds...."*(NIV). This is a command. It is not a passive action, but a deliberate choice to accept and save *only* appropriate and accurate Biblical data.

Romans 12:1 also commands us to, *"not conform any longer to the pattern of the world, but be transformed by the renewing of your mind."* (NIV).

How do we renew our minds?

1. **ENTER** new Godly LIFE-CHANGING information.
2. **MEMORIZE & MEDITATE** on the LIFE-CHANGING Word of God.
3. **PRAY** to God, the LIFE-CHANGER, and ask for His help in the reprogramming or renewing of our minds.

After reading each chapter, take time to evaluate your own thoughts. You may find that you concur with much of what this book states and that it reaffirms what you already believe and embrace. You may, however, find that you must make many adjustments to your present database or thought patterns in order to conform to God's Word. Seek God's help in highlighting areas you need to improve upon.

⌁

This book is divided into two main sections:

Part 1

UNDERSTANDING

Part 2

MEETING

⌁

You need to **UNDERSTAND** (Chapter 1 – 5)

- ♥ How God Views Sex
- ♥ How Your Past Affects Your Present Sexual Life
- ♥ How Men Are Wired
- ♥ How the Seasons of a Marriage Affect Your Sex Life
- ♥ How Men Feel

Before you can proceed to **MEETING** (Chapters 6-8)

- ♥ How to Discuss Your Sexual Relationship with Your Mate
- ♥ How to Plan Your Sex Life
- ♥ How to Make Romance a Part of Every Day

Each chapter of this book is formatted as follows:

LET THE WOMEN SPEAK: These comments represent the feelings and opinions of women I've encountered. Some you will relate to, some you will not.

At the end of each chapter you will find:

LIFE-CHANGING QUESTIONS TO PONDER: These are thought-provoking questions that you should contemplate methodically and thoroughly.

THE LIFE-CHANGING WORD: Read the recommended scriptures repeatedly, and preferably commit them to memory. When you have memorized them, you will be able to recall them at a moment's notice and they will remain permanently in your database or back-up files. Placing these godly thoughts in your long-term memory will allow these new, permanent thought patterns to develop.

Personalize them by inserting your own names, and use them as a basis for your Biblically-based prayers. For example:

> Proverbs 5:19 – *"A loving doe, a graceful deer, may MY*
> _____ *(insert your name), breasts satisfy YOU*
> *always,* _____ *(insert your husband's name), and*
> *may YOU,* _____ *(insert your husband's name), ever*
> *be captivated with MY* _____*(insert your name) love."*
> (NIV – adapted).

By praying the scriptures, you are assured that you are praying in line with God's perfect will. By continually repeating these positive statements of intent, you allow the Word of God to flood into and saturate your mind.

Philippians 4:6 says, *"Pray about everything that concerns you."* (TLB). Your sex life is most definitely a part of your life. Without the least bit of embarrassment, discuss it and other personal concerns with the Lord. If you believe Psalm 139, which states that God is well aware of everything you do, then He already knows each and every concern or activity of your life. There is nothing hidden from Him. Don't allow that fact to be intimidating, but rather, be delighted that the Lord has a special interest in the intimate details of your life. He is most interested in assisting you to become the best woman, lover, and wife you can be.

At the back of the book, you will find several key scriptures to memorize. Photocopy these pages and put these verses in your purse, tape them to your bathroom mirror, leave them by your bedside, or put them inside your daily devotional book for easy and frequent referral. Remember; *only* God's Word can really transform your mind. (See Conclusion, pages 300-304.)

Then, pray to God, the **LIFE-CHANGER**. Take time to express your own feelings based on the chapter contents. You can find great relief from some of the stresses you may have felt regarding your sex life, simply by verbalizing the words and releasing your feelings to God.

Yes, *you have a choice* to make. You can continue to store negative, incorrect thoughts about sexuality or you can choose to enter positive, accurate data that will transform your sex life into something beautiful and exhilarating. Correct sexual thoughts will become correct attitudes, which eventually will become correct actions and new, correct habits.

$\mathscr{A}$n ounce of prevention

is worth a pound of cure.

The fact that you are taking time to reflect on your sexual relationship by reading this book shows that you obviously care a great deal about your relationship with God and your husband. You may not be struggling in this area, or necessarily be dysfunctional. Rather, you have a good marriage that you wish to enrich and enhance.

Caution: It may be that the mere mention of the word "sex" brings painful or sad memories to your mind. Perhaps you are beginning to read this book with great fear and with your internal defenses at full alert. Maybe you still carry deep wounds within because of the abuse of your parents, a boyfriend, or a past mate.

If this is the case, you need to be aware that you will be greatly affected by these thoughts and feelings as you read through this material. These thoughts may affect your response and reaction to the contents of this book, either positively or negatively.

If you have been scarred and wounded by negative sexual experiences which you feel haven't been appropriately dealt with, you may wish to postpone reading the remainder of this book. Seek professional help in working though these areas. Proceed with caution ...Only you know where you are at.

As you read, you will discover that I have shared some of my *own* personal experiences. The way I relate to my husband may *not* appeal to you at all, so do it *your* way – the way that suits *your* personality and the preferences of *your* own unique husband.

Read this book with an open, receptive mind (input data), apply what you think is appropriate for you (save), and disregard (delete) what doesn't suit you or your marriage.

Don't feel pressured to mimic my experience or personality.

God made you special and unique! Be yourself!

A valid criticism of this book could be that little is said regarding the man's responsibility and his role in making a sexual relationship work. This is a correct observation. It takes *two* committed individuals to ensure that an intimate relationship functions well. Men *must* work diligently to understand and meet *our* needs.

That, however, is *not* the focus of this book. This book is directed toward women and their responsibilities *only*. (As I tell the ladies in my seminar, I might have to write a library for the men on how to understand and meet our needs – one book may not be enough!)

So with these thoughts in mind, start reading ...open up your "computer!" Explore and enjoy the process of entering some thought-provoking, perhaps life-changing "data". Your brain is your greatest sex organ. Use it to become the godly, sensuous, exciting lover God intended you to be!

⌒◯⌒

ℛemember ...

Change your thoughts – Change your life!

⌒◯⌒

Ruth

PART ONE

Two-Gether Intimately ...

Understanding Your Husband's Sexual Needs

UNDERSTAND...

Chapter 1   How God Views Sex

Chapter 2   How Your Past Affects Your
                 Present Sexual Life

Chapter 3   How Men Are Wired

Chapter 4   How the Seasons of a Marriage
                 Affect Your Sex Life

Chapter 5   How Men Feel

Chapter One

UNDERSTANDING...

How God Views Sex

*"God Himself invented sex for our
delight. It was His gift to us –
intended for pleasure."*
Ed Wheat, M.D. [1]

Let The Women Speak:

♥ "Does God really OK sex? Isn't sex a carnal practice?"

♥ "I thought sex was only as a result of the fall..."

♥ "I am a new believer and I have never heard anyone talk about it at the church. Is it a taboo?"

♥ "Why do my Christian friends whisper when they talk about sex?"

♥ "Do you think God really expects a couple to enjoy or have fun in their sexual expression, or is it just for making babies?"

♥ "Isn't the sex drive of men equal to the sex drive of animals?"

♥ "Does the Bible really talk about sex? Where does it talk about sex?"

♥ "Isn't sex just a necessary evil – a biological necessity?"

In an age when there seems to be so much talk about sex, there is still much confusion regarding this topic. Many Christians are looking for answers. Much to the amazement of some, the Bible talks very openly about sex and sexuality. It is mentioned in some form in virtually every book of the Bible. Let's take a look at Genesis, where it all began:

Our Sexuality Was Crafted By God

And It Was His Idea

"So God created man in his own image, in the image of God created he him, male and female he created them."
Genesis 1:27 (KJV).

"And God saw all that He had made, and behold, it was <u>very good.</u>" Genesis 1:31 (KJV).

Did you observe the last two words? – *"very good!"* Earlier in the chapter, God had created the fish, the birds, and the animals and said that it was "good," but He reserved the affirmation "very good" for his highest and finest creation. God himself personally and lovingly created the human body and was very pleased with this accomplishment.

Notice the verse says, *"He created man in his <u>own</u> image."* (KJV). God created animals, male and female, and they breed according to instinct with God-given biological motivation. Yet humans are different in that they not only use their bodies to procreate, but also to enjoy a personal, emotional, and spiritual relationship with their mates.

Even the sex act itself reminds us that its goal is to bring together two people. It is no coincidence that man is the only one of God's creations who relates sexually face-to-face. 2

There were so many things in the Garden of Eden that God created good and considered very good – but we read later, in Genesis 2:18, that something was *"not good."*

> *"And the Lord God said, It is <u>not good</u> that the man should be alone; I will make him a <u>help meet</u> suitable for him."*
>
> *" And the Lord God caused a deep sleep to fall upon Adam, and he took one of his ribs, and closed up his flesh instead thereof; And the rib, which the Lord God had taken from man, made he a woman, and brought her unto the man. And Adam said, This is now bone of my bones, and flesh of my flesh: she shall be called Woman, because she was taken out of Man."*
> Genesis 2: 21- 23 (KJV).

One can only imagine the delight and surprise when Adam woke up from his nap. He may have shouted with glee, "Wow-man!" as he stood transfixed, gazing at his new beautiful partner.

Observing that Adam was alone and that he needed companionship, the Lord created Eve, a friend and lover who was capable of providing emotional, spiritual, and physical intimacy.

God lovingly created this unique friend, not to *compete* with man but to *complete* him. According to God, woman was designed to be man's helper. The term 'helper' refers to a beneficial relationship where one person aids and supports another person. Perhaps some may think of a helper as a subordinate, a kind of glorified servant, but here God refers to a *valued* friend and ally.[3] (Note: saying this, however, does not imply that a woman cannot be her own person with goals, values, and plans. She is a separate, unique entity. However, if she chooses to marry, *one* of her roles will be to meet her husband's needs and support him.)

This description of women is clarified when you note that the same Hebrew word for 'help' is used of God Himself in Psalms 46:1, where He is called our Helper, *"a very present help in trouble."* (KJV).[4]

$\mathcal{R}$emember ...

Change your thoughts – Change your life!

37

Genesis 2:24 still remains the most concise and comprehensive counseling session ever presented on marriage... leave, cleave, and unite.

Following the creation of Eve, the Lord gives Adam a brief counselling session outlining how he should relate to his new bride. Genesis 2:24 remains the most concise and comprehensive counselling session ever presented on marriage. It is made up of twenty-two easily understood words containing a wealth of meaning.

First, Genesis 2:24 says, *"Therefore shall a man leave his father and his mother..."* (KJV).

The Bible commands us that we should stop being dependent on our parents. While we should always maintain a loving bond and respect for our parents, this relationship must change after marriage in order to ensure full commitment to our spouse. Together, the husband and wife are to create a new home.

Second, Genesis 2:24 continues, *"and shall cleave unto his wife"* (KJV).

© *John McPherson (Used by permission)*

The word 'cleaving' in this sense means to be "welded inseparably, to adhere, to be attached by a strong tie, to cement together, hold fast to," so that each becomes a part of the other. There is nothing passive about cleaving to one's partner.[5]

And third, 2:24 states, *"And they shall be one flesh"* (KJV).

Adam was commanded to be joined together in sexual union. This joining together implies not only the joining of two bodies, but of soul and spirit as well.

Genesis 2:25 states, *"And they were both naked, the man and his wife, and were not ashamed"* (KJV).

The Hebrew term 'naked' is translated 'laid bare.' [6] This original couple was unhindered emotionally as well as physically, and they experienced maximum freedom

39

together. Adam and Eve could see each other as they really were – without disappointment or fear. They did not experience any self-consciousness about their nakedness, and their blissful state was without sin or shame.

They revelled in a childlike trust and curiosity – laughing, exploring, giving, and receiving love. Their sexuality was a glorious and innocent celebration lived out with honesty, respect, and a great deal of zest.[7]

**If anyone has made you feel *unspiritual*
because you believe
sex is created and blessed of God
for mutual enjoyment
then set them straight! They are wrong!
Christians need to claim, sanctify, and celebrate
the wonder and enjoyment of their sexuality.
God says it is *very good* – and so should we!** [8]

Sexuality Was Designed By God

For Procreation

Genesis 1:28 introduces His idea of sexual intimacy for reproduction: *"And God blessed them saying, Be fruitful, and multiply and replenish the earth..."* (KJV). This is certainly one commandment that man has chosen to obey through the years - sometimes in an extravagant way!

In the case of a healthy male and female, God has endowed us with the appropriate sexual body parts to enable this miracle to occur.

Psalms 139:14 states that *"we are fearfully and wonderfully made – marvelous are thy works!"* (KJV). One must stand in awe that God would choose to use *our* physical bodies to reproduce His creative masterpiece.

"THERE! YOU FELT IT KICK THAT TIME, DIDN'T YOU?"

© John McPherson (Used by permission)

Some mistakenly believe that once children are born, sexual intimacy has served its purpose – "a necessary evil," as some people have called it. Yet God's plan for intimacy between married partners is much broader than a biological necessity.

Sexuality Was Designed By God

For Recreation & Personal Pleasure

The Book of Proverbs develops the idea that sexual intimacy was created for personal pleasure as well as procreation.

> *"Drink from your own well, my son – be faithful and true to your wife. Why should you beget children with women of the street? Why share your children with those outside your home? Let your manhood be a blessing; rejoice in the wife of your youth. Let her charms and tender embrace satisfy you. Let her love alone fill you with delight!"* Proverbs 5:15-20 (TLB).

It would be difficult to conclude from this passage that God is some sort of puritanical prude who scowls at sexual enjoyment. He desires that marriage should provide us with ecstatic sexual delights that are exhilarating and pleasurable!

Sex is *not* only for procreation – but for *recreation!*

"God Himself invented sex for our delight. It was His gift to us – intended for pleasure." [9]

The Song of Solomon, a romantic love poem, clearly delineates a wonderful sexual relationship between a man and his wife. Some Christians take offense when it is suggested that these very intimate encounters between a man and his wife refer to their very pleasurable sexual relations. They would suggest that it is a symbolic statement about God and His love for us. Though they may view this book as an allegory illustrating the love relationship between Christ and the church, it can most certainly be read at face value. It is the intimate and amorous conversation of Solomon and the Shulamite woman, a couple deeply in love.

"Just kidding … just kidding!
I'm really not preaching on
Song of Solomon today."

© *Steve Phelps (Used by permission)*

This passage is not "X-rated" material, but it is a highly sensuous, yet wholesome love poem that God chose to include in His Holy Scriptures.

Let's look specifically at a few passages...

Song of Solomon 1:2 – *"Let him kiss me with the kisses of his mouth – for your love is more delightful than wine. Pleasing is the fragrance of your perfumes; your name is like perfume poured out. No wonder the maidens love you! Take me away with you – let us hurry."*

1:15-16 – *"How beautiful you are, my darling! Oh, how beautiful! Your eyes are doves. How handsome you are, my lover! Oh, how charming! And our bed is verdant."*

5:10-12 – *"My lover is radiant and ruddy, outstanding among ten thousand. His head is purest gold; his hair is wavy and black as a raven. His eyes are like doves by the water streams, washed in milk, mounted like jewels. His cheeks are like beds of spice yielding perfume. His lips are like lilies dripping with myrrh. His arms are rods of gold set with chrysolite. His body is like polished ivory decorated with sapphires. His legs are pillars of marble set on bases of pure gold. His appearance is like Lebanon, choice as its cedars. His mouth is sweetness itself, he is altogether lovely. This is my lover, this my friend."*

7:1 – *"How beautiful your sandaled feet, O prince's daughter! Your graceful legs are like jewels, the work of a craftsman's hands. Your navel is a rounded goblet that never lacks blended wine. Your waist is a mount of wheat encircled by lilies. Your breasts are like two fawns, twins of a gazelle. Your neck is like an ivory tower..."*

7:6 – *"How beautiful you are and how pleasing, O love, with your delights."*

7:7-8a – *"Your stature is like that of the palm, and your breasts like clusters of fruit. I said, 'I will climb the palm tree; I will take hold of its fruit.' "* (Does this sound familiar, girls?)

7:8b-11 – *"May your breasts be like the clusters of the vine, the fragrance of your breath like apples, and your mouth like the best wine. May the wine go straight to my lover, flowing gently over lips and teeth. I belong to my lover, and his desire is for me. Come, my lover, let us go to the countryside, let us spend the night in the villages."*

8:3 – *"His left arm is under my head and his right arm embraces me."*

8:14 – *"Come away, my lover, and be like a gazelle or like a young stag on the spice laden mountains..."* (NIV).

From reading these passages, one can sense the appreciation these lovers had for each other's bodies and the sheer excitement and appreciation they felt about being together.

These scriptures certainly endorse sexual pleasure within marriage. This is a concept that many Christian women struggle with. They can accept the fact that God crafted sexuality, but they certainly feel guilty when they actually revel in and enjoy their sexuality. Many women who have attended my seminars have shared comments such as these:

"I just can't give myself permission to enjoy my sexual relations with my husband."

"I believe God only tolerates this 'carnal pleasure,' but He doesn't really want me to delight in it."

"I feel that somehow I am disappointing God when I entertain sexual fantasies about my husband and me."

"I don't think I can be godly and sensuous at the same time."

Why can't these women give themselves permission to pursue the sensuous pleasures of married love?

"ARE YOU SURE THIS IS THE HONEYMOON SUITE?"

© *John McPherson (Used by permission)*

Because they feel that being godly and sensuous simultaneously is unattainable. They have a distorted definition of what sensuous means.[10]

Webster's Dictionary defines the word 'sensuous' as "pertaining to the senses, alive to the pleasure to be received through the senses."[11] This term has a desirable, positive meaning. Secular culture has somehow tainted this term with negative, provocative connotations by referring to unrestrained sexual appetite whenever and with whomever they please. Because the media has so radically distorted God's idea of sex, many ladies feel they must disassociate themselves from anything erotic or sensuous in order to be godly. This is, of course, wrong.

Those who envision sex as "ungodly" or "less than spiritual" often use verses such as Galatians 5:15 (NIV):

> *"Live by the Spirit, and you will not gratify the desires of the sinful nature,"* or, *"Set your minds on things above, not on earthly things,"* Colossians 3:2 (NIV).

These verses do not refer to sexual pleasures, but rather to selfish, ungodly pursuits. Many women in their intense desire to be "spiritual" and "godly" often compartmentalize their lives in the following way:

The "Halo" Compartment

(Her Spiritual Self)

These are the times when she is praying, reading the Word, or engaging in church activities and service. She feels it is only during these times that she is really pleasing God and doing His highest and holy will. *(See Figure 1.)*

The "Homemaking" Compartment

(Her Physical Self)

These are the times when she is doing housework, laundry, diapers, or secular work. She sees these as necessary evils, only acceptable in God's sight because they support or make possible her time when she is spiritual.

The "Hedonistic" Compartment

(Her Carnal Self)

These are the times when she is enjoying some aspect of life: leisure, sports, vacation, and yes - her sexual pleasures with her husband. She feels God tolerates these activities, but He really would prefer if she would be more serious and more dedicated to the *higher* purposes in life.

**The "Halo"
Compartment**
(Spiritual Self)
Prayer, Bible Study, Service

**The "Homemaking"
Compartment**
(Physical Self)
Childcare, Housework

**The "Hedonistic"
Compartment**
(Carnal Self)
Sex, Pleasure, Leisure

Figure 1

This type of compartmentalization is contrary to God's Word. Colossians 3:2 indicates that all of life is sacred and we are to do *everything* heartily as unto the Lord. Our spiritual, physical, and sexual selves should all fuse together and be fully integrated. 12

God's Word says ALL of life is sacred.
We are to do everything as unto the Lord,
from the changing of diapers to our sexual
relationship.

"For everything created by God is good, and nothing is to be rejected, if it is received with gratitude; for it is sanctified by means of the word of God and prayer."
I Timothy 4:4-5 (NIV).

"Everything lives by his power, and everything is for his glory. To him be glory evermore." Romans 11:36 (TLB).
'EVERYTHING' INCLUDES YOUR SEXUALITY!

*ℛ*emember ...

Change your thoughts – Change your life!

© Jerry Cogan (Used by permission)

This is a crucial change of thinking that many Christian women have to embrace if they are going to really enjoy *all* the pleasures of marital love that God intended.

Sex Was Designed To Be Enjoyed Only In The Confines Of A Marital Relationship

This is a thought that is foreign to many living in our contemporary society. Wife-swapping, cohabitation, adultery, premarital sex, homosexuality, and so forth - all of these at times seem to be the accepted norm, although none of these practices are approved by God. Our culture is saturated with sex; love has been

distorted by lust, and God-given boundaries are ignored.
God makes it clear that sexual intimacy is to be enjoyed
by marriage partners *only.*

> *"But since there is so much immorality, each man
> should have his <u>own</u> wife, and each woman her <u>own</u>
> husband. The husband should fulfill his marital duty to
> his wife, and likewise the wife to her husband."*
> I Corinthians 7:2-3 (NIV).

"I HAVEN'T GOTTEN TO THAT PART YET!"

© *John McPherson (Used by permission)*

Sexuality Is Viewed By God As Being Honorable, Beautiful, And Wholesome

Hebrews 13:4 says, *"Marriage should be <u>honored</u> by all,
and the marriage bed kept pure, for God will judge the
adulterer and all the sexually immoral."* (NIV).

A modern-day version of this might read, "We must
have a very high view of marriage; what goes on in the

marriage bed is wholesome, respectable, and healthy..." God assures us that the marriage bed is to be held in great honor and sexual relations can take place within marriage in a guilt-free and uninhibited manner.

Since God uses our sexual relationship as a word picture of His love for us, it should not be construed as inappropriate, carnal.

$\mathcal{S}$exual Intimacy Is A Mutual Right And Responsibility Of Each Married Partner

> I Corinthians 7:4 states, *"The wife's body <u>does not belong to her alone</u> but also to her husband. In the same way, the husband's body does not belong to him alone but also to his wife."* (NIV).

Both wife and husband have conjugal rights and exclusive possession of each other's body. This does *not* imply that partners can misuse, disrespect, or abuse their mates for their own selfish gratification, but rather that each partner would recognize that their bodies do not belong to themselves *alone*. A partner has the *right and privilege* of enjoying the other's body unreservedly.

$\mathcal{S}$exual Intimacy Is To Be Uninterrupted

> *"Do not deprive each other except by <u>mutual consent</u> and <u>for a time</u>, so that you may devote yourselves to prayer. <u>Then come together again</u> so that Satan will not tempt you because of your lack of self-control."*
> I Corinthians 7:5 (NIV).

This passage teaches us that sexual relations between a couple are not to be restrained or squelched, except for some *rare* exceptions. These exceptions should be:

First, by *mutual agreement.* Second, because of wishing to spend *extra quality time in prayer.* Third, *only in a temporary* situation and not for long periods of time.

Some individuals, whom I have dubbed "pseudo saints," often excuse themselves from meeting their partner's sexual needs for long periods of time because they find themselves doing "more spiritual things." If they are excusing their lack of creative love because they are so involved in a plethora of spiritual activities, they have made a disastrous choice. No amount of Bible study, church attendance, or acts of Christian service can negate the *need* and *responsibility* to cultivate physical love in our relationship with our marriage partner. The ministries of many Christians have been undermined by this neglect of Biblical priorities.

"I don't care if it *is* the armor of God. You take it off or go sleep on the couch."

© *Rob Portlock (Used by permission)*

Some people view sex as a pleasure they should deny themselves in lieu of other more important acts of service to God. This type of thinking is *contrary* to God's Word. It is the couple whose relationship is based on the will and Word of God who should have a meaningful and fulfilling romantic life.

If you are married, God has called you to meet the sexual needs of your husband as a top priority and it should be viewed as an essential part of your ministry to your husband. Do not justify your lack of sexual interest and devotion by pursuing other legitimate, but secondary, religious activities.

> In Matthew 19:4-6 we are told, *"Haven't you read?"* He replied, *"that at the beginning the Creator made them male and female, and said, 'For this reason a man will leave his father and mother and be united to his wife, and the two will become one flesh. So they are no longer two, but one.' Therefore what God has joined together, let man not separate."* (NIV).

Here, Jesus reinforces the fact that a man and his wife should be one flesh (engage in sexual intercourse) and that this bond should hold them together. Christian couples have the capacity to enjoy maximum sexual enjoyment as their union represents not only the joining of two physical bodies, but a spiritual and emotional union as well.

Conclusion

One can see from the above that our Creator and His Word *strongly*

ENDORSES sexual intimacy...

ENCOURAGES sexual intimacy...

EXPECTS sexual intimacy to be

ENJOYED...

and to be an *ENDEARING, EXCITING, EXHILARATING*

part of a growing marriage.

Life-Changing Questions to Ponder

❤ Do you still struggle with accepting the fact that God crafted sexuality?

❤ Are you willing to release and replace other wrong or incorrect thoughts in this regard?

❤ Have you taken time to identify where your incorrect thinking has originated? Who has influenced your thinking inappropriately? Do you need to stop listening to those voices?

The Life-Changing Word...
Memorize/Meditate

"Marriage should be honored by all, and the marriage bed kept pure..." Hebrew 13:4 (NIV).

♦ ♦ ♦

"For this reason a man will leave his father and mother and be united to his wife, and the <u>two will become one. flesh.</u>" Matthew 19:4 (NIV).

♥ Do you accept the fact that God created you *female* and that it was His plan for you?

♥ Do you find yourself resenting the fact that He created you female instead of male?

♥ Can you identify any reasons why you would resent being female? Have you received some wrong messages regarding this from family members, peers, or a mate?

♥ Do you have to repent for your lack of acceptance of the gender God created you to be?

The Life-Changing Word...
Memorize/Meditate

"I am fearfully and wonderfully made (A female) ...
Your works are <u>wonderful</u>."
Psalms 139:14 (NIV adapted).

♦ ♦ ♦

"So God created man in his own image, in the image of God
He created him male and female He created them...and
behold it was <u>very good</u>." Genesis 1:27 & 31 (KJV).

♥ Do you see yourself as a "very good" creation of God? Are there some self-esteem issues you need to address? How do you think God views you? If you don't see yourself as a valuable, lovable, unique creation of God –

this is definitely going to affect how you relate to your husband.

♥ Do you have difficulty accepting the fact that God created women to be "helpmates" for men? Do you resent this fact? Do you view this as a subservient, menial role? Do you need to redefine your role in marriage?

The Life-Changing Word...
Memorize/Meditate

> *"He who finds a wife finds what is <u>good</u> and receives favor from the Lord."* Proverbs 18:22 (NIV).
>
> ♦ ♦ ♦
>
> *"It is not good that man should be alone, I will make him a help meet suitable for him."*
> Genesis 2:18 (KJV).

♥ Do you feel that you and your husband have been released to form a new home? Are either of you still connected to the "apron strings" of your parents in an unhealthy way? If yes, do you understand how this could affect your marital and sexual relationship?

♥ Would you agree that you are actively pursing this act of cleaving as defined earlier in the book, or are you rather passive about this activity? Do you need to change your priorities?

The Life-Changing Word...
Memorize/Meditate

> *"Therefore shall a man <u>leave</u> his mother and father, and shall <u>cleave</u> to his wife and they shall be <u>one flesh</u>."*
> Genesis 2:24 (NIV).

♥ Have you read Song of Solomon lately – slowly and methodically in a modern translation?

♥ Have you really grasped the excitement and passionate lovemaking between these two people?

♥ Can you say that the situation is similar in your own home? Why or why not?

♥ Have you compartmentalized your life? Halo/ Homemaking/Hedonistic Self?

♥ Do you believe you can be sensuous and spiritual simultaneously?

♥ Do you believe in theory and in practice that sexual intimacy is the mutual right and responsibility of each married partner? Do you resist or resent your responsibility or rights? Why?

The Life-Changing Word...
Memorize/Meditate

"The wife's body does not belong to her alone but also to her husband." I Corinthians 7:3 (NIV).

♦ ♦ ♦

- The Book of Song of Solomon

❤ Have you been depriving your mate of regular sexual relations? Why?

❤ Do you feel you are exposing your mate to great temptation in this area?

❤ Have you been putting other perhaps noble, maybe "spiritual," activities before the priority of meeting your husband's needs?

My Prayer to the
Life-Changer

Dear God: After reading this chapter, I...

_____

_____

_____

_____

Chapter Two

UNDERSTANDING...

How Your Past Affects Your Present Sexual Life

"You cannot change your past,
but you can sure
change your future."
Author Unknown

Let The Women Speak:

- ♥ "I am so angry with my husband while we're in bed. I feel when he touches me, that all the horrible memories of my past come between us."

- ♥ "I had a baby out of wedlock. Even though I am a Christian now, I still feel I can never achieve the spirituality I long for, because I am still condemned for my past."

- ♥ "I can't forgive my father for sexually abusing me as a child. He has ruined my life. The scars of his abuse just don't seem to heal."

- ♥ "Memories of my two abortions still haunt me. In both instances, I was pressured by my boyfriend and my parents. I regret my decision greatly. I can't seem to forgive myself and get over it."

- ♥ "I was very promiscuous in the days before my salvation. I slept with almost all of the boys in town in an effort to gain their love and acceptance. They all ended up ditching me and I now feel used, bitter, and abandoned."

♥ "Every man in my life has used me and then told me I was stupid and useless. Now that I am married, I have great difficulty really believing my husband when he says he loves me and accepts me. I just can't seem to trust him because of my past negative experiences with men."

♥ "I cheated on my husband. He doesn't know about it. At times, the guilt is unbearable. I don't think he or God could ever forgive me."

♥ "My father was a demanding, verbally abusive, bossy dictator. I find that I have trouble submitting to my husband's loving leadership. I still feel anger against my father because of his treatment of me."

𝒯he Scars of the Past

All of us carry memories of things we wish we could change about our past. Perhaps we made some poor choices during a rebellious period in our teens, or maybe we made some deliberate choices as an adult that we now regret. Often these experiences occurred before we knew the Lord, perhaps during a time when we weren't aware of God's perspective or His directives on these issues.

Some women are forced to carry the pain of negative sexual experiences over which they had no control. As children or in their teens, they may have been abused by a parent, relative, or boyfriend and forced to participate in sexual acts against their will. The scars remain.

Whatever the circumstances, the fact is that the past has left some ladies scarred and wounded. They now, because of their past, have an inability to develop intimacy with their mates or enjoy a fulfilling sex life.

If these instances reflect any of your thoughts, then you should consider how those issues outside of the bedroom or from your past are now affecting your present sexual life. Perhaps this analogy will be helpful.

Having unresolved issues is like having a beach ball deep within. If you have ever played with a beach ball in a pool or lake, you know that in order to keep the ball submerged, it requires a great deal of energy and concentration. The moment you do not focus your energy on keeping it underwater, it immediately rises to the surface.

One lady shared, "Whenever I get into bed with my husband, I feel so angry that I want to explode. I realize that it is not because my husband is doing anything wrong. It is the fact that I have such hatred against men because of past experiences. Whenever my husband tries to be intimate with me, a "volcano" erupts from deep within me and consequently I pour my "hot, molten ash" all over him. I hate myself for hurting my husband with my caustic, scathing words and accompanying unloving actions, but I don't know what to do."

I explained to her that she may have an inner "beach ball" of unresolved bitterness, anger, and resentment. Whenever she lets her guard down, those feelings spew out of her mouth in a forceful, hateful manner.

Until she chooses to deal with those issues, she will be required to use a great deal of energy hiding her "fuming volcano of hurts" within. Because these feelings are so volatile, they may surface at a moment's notice and sometimes are triggered by the least little thing. Often her confused, bewildered husband will ask himself what provoked this offensive verbal assault. He may be unaware of the great wounds she hides beneath her beautiful, smiling face.

So what is the answer?

1. Recognize that there are negative sexual issues in your past.

2. Recognize how they are affecting your present sexual life.

3. Seek the help you need: God, the Bible, a trusted friend, or a professional Christian counsellor.

Notice the order I have suggested. Always take your problems and concerns to the great Counsellor, Healer, Transformer, Forgiver, God, *first*. He knows you better than you know yourself and better than any counsellor could ever hope to. Pour out your concerns verbally or write a letter to Him. Ask the Holy Spirit to come and heal the wounds you carry within. He would delight in freeing you from the chains of guilt, regret, and shame that now bind you. Seek out the Scriptures that will assist you in dealing with your struggles. His Word can speak to your every need. Spend concerted times of studying, fasting, and prayer. God can and will, at times, supernaturally heal wounds that should have taken months or years to heal.

On other occasions, however, He will choose to use loving, caring people and or professionals to help you process your past and embrace the health He so desperately desires you to have.

Why Some Don't Go for Help

If you are still struggling with accepting the fact that you need help, perhaps this fictitious story will help you.

I love to powerwalk and I regularly walk around the perimeter of our town near a wooded area. Let's imagine that one day I am on my powerwalk when suddenly a very disturbed, angry individual jumps from behind some trees and tackles me, knocking me to the ground. There he proceeds to punch, kick, cut, and hurt me deeply. Immediately after, he flees away, leaving me wounded, bruised, and terrified on the edge of the path. While crying with the pain, I manage to drag myself home and flop my bleeding body at the front entrance of our home.

Simon, my husband, hearing my distress comes running to see what is wrong. Through my tears, I tell him what happened and he does his best to lovingly assure me that I will be all right and that he will do everything in his power to help me. He shares with me that he can't imagine the emotional and physical pain I must be feeling, but he assures me by saying, "Don't worry dear, I'll never leave your side until you are totally healed. I'm here for you and will be with you through this very difficult and distressful time."

After assessing my wounds, Simon announces that he will be carrying me to our car and taking me to the hospital for the medical attention I require.

Instead of willingly agreeing to his request, I shout back at him, "No way! I will not go! Leave me alone!"

Simon, with a look of disbelief, might ask, "Why would you refuse this help? I want to help you, I love you, I can't see you suffer like this ...."

Why might I refuse help? Let's explore a few possibilities:

1. I Do Not Want To Face The Embarrassment

I know that when I go to the doctor, he will ask me many questions and undoubtedly call the police to interrogate me with more. Perhaps I don't want to admit that I was assaulted in this manner. I don't want others to know. Fearing what they will think and say, I decide this situation must be kept "hush hush," with only my family aware of the details.

2. I Don't Want To Face More Pain

It may be necessary for the doctor to "inflict" more pain as he treats my injuries. I may require many painful stitches, needles, realignments, or even minor surgery. I am convinced that all of these procedures are going to be painful, and there is no way I will allow myself to be hurt further.

3. I Am Too Proud

My father may have raised me to believe that our family should *never* have to ask for help. He strongly affirmed, "If we were down to our last penny, we would *never* admit it. We can solve *all* problems ourselves. We are strong; we don't need anybody at anytime!"

My hesitation in getting help might be rooted in this inability to be vulnerable and ask for assistance. I've learned that I can never ask for help.

4. I Am Very Skeptical About The Help I Might Receive From Health Professionals

Perhaps I went to a doctor after another accident I experienced and he didn't set a fracture correctly. I resolved that I would never set foot in a doctor's office again. Because of this one unfortunate occurrence, I will never allow myself to be in the care of anyone in the medical profession. Simple as that!

5. I Am Too Angry

I am paralyzed with such rage and hatred, that I just do not have enough energy to deal with yet another stressful situation.

So what is Simon to do? I am a full-grown adult who is screaming, kicking, and vehemently arguing against any need for more help.

1. He could call, against my will, for the ambulance. They might come with a straitjacket or sedate me and take me to the hospital. Because I was so intent on not going to the hospital, I might wait for the first opportunity to remove the IV and slip past the nurse's station to come home. Or, if forced to stay, I could refuse to take any of the medication, or allow the staff to cleanse my wounds, and I might recoil from any therapy they offered me. Despite the fact that Simon brought me to this institution which could help me greatly, if I am not in the state of mind to accept this help, there is not a great deal the medical staff or Simon can do for me.

2. After great effort and much frustration, he could finally give up and say "Okay, Ruth, have it your own way! Lie on the floor and fix this problem yourself. I have done everything possible to help you, but you continue to resist further assistance – so just stay there!"

    So what are the likely consequences to either of the above choices?

I am left in my pain to suffer. I am the one who will remain a wounded, handicapped person unable to live the fulfilling life I would desire. If these wounds are not attended to quickly, I could realize permanent damage to my body, infection could set in, and I could experience many other complications.

This fact would be unfortunate enough in itself, but I must admit to another reality. Because of my refusal to seek help, I am not going to be able to be the wife I desire to be, the loving mother I long to be, the effective Christian I could be. Other people and ultimately the Lord's kingdom are going to suffer because of my refusal to deal with my past.

So what am I trying to say?

Yes, as in this story, you may have had wounds inflicted upon you by others. It was not my fault that, in my hypothetical scenario, the man beat me up and hurt me deeply. It maybe was not your fault that you were abused. You may truly be a victim. You may feel that you have had to go through life encumbered with "baggage" you would have never chosen to carry. You may feel very embarrassed and enraged with God for allowing such events to occur.

Perhaps, because of the nature of the wound, you have never been given permission to verbalize the abuse. You might have been threatened that if you ever opened your mouth, your life would be in danger. The verbal, emotional, and mental abuse you have endured has left your self-esteem at an all-time low. At times, you wonder if you can ever feel normal and happy, and if you can be the loving wife that you so long to be.

No One Understands

Perhaps you think that no one knows how you feel. You are quite correct. Pain in these areas is of a personal and intimate nature. Only you can understand the depth of that pain. You may have been annoyed at people who have tried to pretend that they understood. Having someone who has never been in your circumstances say, "I know how you feel," is like someone who has never given birth standing beside you in the delivery room saying, "I know just how you feel; The pain is really nothing; what's your problem? It can't be that bad."

Now what about your response? Why might you refuse help?

1. **You're Right. It Will Be Embarrassing To Uncover Some of the Details Of Your Past, Either to Yourself, Your Spouse, Your Pastor, or A Counsellor.**

The details of your horrible experiences may never have been verbalized by you to anyone. You have worked very hard at burying them deep within, fearing that people will think less of you if they become aware that you have had problems in your past. You fear their ridicule or even their rejection and think they will turn the situation around and blame you, saying it must have been your fault.

All of these feelings are common and are to be expected. However, what are the consequences of not facing your embarrassment?

You are left wounded and handicapped. You will never become the beautiful, whole person God wants you to be.

2. You're Right. It Will Be Painful To Talk About Your Past.

It may take you days and many tears to share with God, a trusted friend, or a counsellor the details you choose to relate. Uncovering and healing the wretched past may be an unbelievably arduous and difficult task. No doubt about that.

The statement "No pain, no gain" may apply here. Just as it would be temporarily painful for me to have minor surgery or daily therapy to help my body function properly again, it may be temporarily painful for you to sift through your past as you move through the healing process.

Wanting to avoid pain is a natural instinct. However, what are the consequences of not facing your pain?

You are left wounded. You will never become the beautiful, whole person God intended you to be.

3. Your Pride Is Standing In Your Way

You have difficulty admitting your inadequacy. It may be as a result of your training during your formative years. If so, you may avoid admitting problems at any cost.

The Lord had no reluctance in sharing His loving concern for people with areas of need. He said to His disciples, "Look fellows, the healthy don't need a doctor, I have come to reach out and bring healing to the wounded. My mission is to help the wounded in any way possible to realize their full potential." (Mark 2:17 - my paraphrase).

Jeremiah 29:11 reads, *"For I know the plans I have for you,"* declares the Lord, *"plans to prosper you and not to harm you, plans to give you hope and a future."* (NIV).

If someone has wrongly programmed you to think that it is a sign of weakness to ask for help, then that is some data you need to "delete" from your internal computer. You must, however, be the one to choose to hit the delete button. If you continue to choose to store this painful data, then you will suffer the consequences. In summary,

You can choose to reject any help – but in doing so, you will restrict the Lord from working in your life, and you will not become the beautiful person He wants you to be.

4. You Had A Negative Experience With A Pastor Or Counsellor

Perhaps this person gave you an incorrect diagnosis or some inappropriate counsel. You may be right on this issue. They could have been wrong. You may feel anger toward that counsellor and have resolved to never go to another one again. Because one person made a mistake, however, it is not fair to assume that all counsellors are incompetent. If you choose to forgive this person for the hurts you feel that he/she has inflicted on you, you will find that healing occurs and you will be able to trust again.

If you choose to refuse help because of a negative experience with a counsellor, then you will have to solve your problem on your own, without the use of some significant resources. Why not start utilizing additional resources such as: books and professionals? What have you got to lose?

> *You can yet become the beautiful person*
> *that God wants you to become.*

5. You Are Still So Livid And Angry Over The Situation That You Can't Deal With Your Past

You may need someone to listen to you as you scream out your true feelings. You need to vent and put your real emotions in full view, with no threat of judgment or an ensuing lecture.

You can keep all of these negative (and mostly legitimate) feelings pent up or you can let the "inner volcano" be diffused by choosing to trust people who will listen and help. They will point you to Christ, who can help you release you from your anger.

Yes, you may feel angry, but how long do you intend to remain so? When is enough enough?

> *You must become the beautiful person*
> *God intended you to be.*

You will have noted that I am continually urging you to consider the consequences of your choices. Failure to honestly accept the consequences of your choices keeps you in a delusional, helpless victim state.

I remember hearing a lady share an experience on a radio talk show. One night, she stopped on the side of the road to help a man that appeared to be having car trouble. Instead, he tackled her, threw her into the deep ditch by the side of the road, and proceeded to rape her. (I can't think of too many things that would be more horrifying.) She continued to share that after she talked this whole experience through with her loving husband, her caring Pastor and her helpful doctor, she made a decision. She said, "That horrible man stole my personal happiness on that day and for several weeks to follow, but he will steal from me *no more.* By choosing to forgive him and releasing myself from the anger and rage that I feel toward him, I will put closure to this experience. I refuse to let this violent man continue to intrude into my life and give me nightmares. I will not give him that much power over me."

I remember listening intently to this woman's story as I drove in my car. At that moment, I prayed to the Lord that should a similar incident ever happen to me, I would respond in the same manner. Her gutsy, courageous stand made me feel like stopping the car and giving her a standing ovation. Did she make the right choice? Of course she did. Some women years later, would still have been crying over the fact that they had been raped and would have been willing to recount the play-by-play description of that terrible situation.

This woman did not choose to deny that it happened, nor did she avoid seeking professional help. She CHOSE to put a period there. "This incident will not rob me of any of my future happiness or potential to be what God wants me to be. God will help me to be an overcomer!"

Undoubtedly, you have heard the saying, "You need to forgive and forget." I don't agree with this statement. Unless the Lord would strike her with amnesia, how could she *forget* the horrifying memories of this experience? No, she would choose to *remember*, but would choose to let *go* of the hurt.

Joseph, in the book of Genesis, is a superb example of this. He certainly did not forget that his angry brothers had maliciously sold him to be a slave in Egypt, but he chose to forgive and let go of his hurts and bitterness. (Genesis 45)

Consider these quotes:

"You cannot change your past, but you can sure change your future." (Author Unknown)

That's right! There isn't one thing you can do to change what has already transpired in your life – but you certainly have the power to change your future.

"Most people are about as happy as they choose to be." (Abraham Lincoln)

You can choose to wallow in your past or you can choose to work through it methodically and get on with your life.

Unforgiveness is like having a videotape in your memory. Because you have chosen not to forgive, you rewind and replay the painful details over and over again. When you forgive, you begin to heal the hurt associated with those old videotapes in your memory and...

Become the beautiful, whole person
that God intended you to be.

ℐ Can't Forgive Myself

Perhaps, unlike the example above you were not a victim. You might say, "I was plain stupid. I, by my own unwise choices, have created my own circumstances." Others might say, "I can't forgive myself for letting my boyfriend talk me into sex when I was only 17," or "I can't forgive myself for having that abortion." "I can't forgive myself for cheating on my husband." "I can't forgive ..." (you fill in the blank).

Yes, you may have done some things you now regret and maybe you have had to suffer some unpleasant consequences, but are you going to let these past mistakes stifle and ruin your future?

Reflect on these encouraging words:

The Lord forgives you. 1 John 1:9 states, *"If we confess our sins, He is faithful and just to forgive our sins and cleanse us from ALL unrighteousness."* (KJV). (Note the word *ALL,* that certainly includes whatever you have done.) I recall one lady responding, "Oh, but Ruth, you don't know how many evil things I have done," and my response was, "I don't care how many inappropriate things you think you have done. If you have chosen to ask God's forgiveness, then choose to believe His Word. *"As far as the east is from the west",* that's how far he has removed your sins and He has put them in His sea of forgetfulness (Psalm 103:12) (KJV). And He has posted a sign: *"No Fishing!"* If you continue to remind yourself of these past issues...

You will never become the beautiful,
whole woman of God He wants you to be.

I questioned one lady whether she assumed any of the wrong things she had done to be as evil as those of a mass murderer. She said, "No, it certainly wasn't that bad." I took her to scriptures where the Apostle Paul admits to having Christians tortured and murdered during the first century. He admits, *"Christ came to save sinners of which I am the greatest!"* (I Timothy 1:15) (NIV). If Paul could choose to embrace the forgiveness of God, then so can you! It is a choice!

David would be another excellent example. He committed adultery with Bathsheba and then schemed to have her husband murdered in order to cover up his sin. Those actions were very evil, but as you will read in Psalm 51, he confessed his sin to God and the Bible later refers to him as a man after God's own heart. (Acts 13:22) (KJV). If God can forgive and restore David, He can certainly forgive you!

You have to *choose* to accept this truth.

Were there consequences to David's actions? Yes, and there always are consequences to sin. But that doesn't mean you can't accept those consequences and continue to mature in your Christian walk. It may be time to delete and edit some of your past incorrect thinking. Choose to believe God's Word.

P.S. If you think other Christians, your parents, or your friends have never forgiven you, then that is *their* problem. God says that if they don't forgive you, He won't forgive them (Matthew 6:14) (NIV). Choose to leave their lack of forgiveness with the Lord and ask Him to work in their lives. You can't let their response slow you down…

In becoming the beautiful and whole person
He desires you to be.

After reading this chapter, you may say, "I need to stop right here. The rest of the book will not be helpful to me at this time. Before I can really understand and meet my husband's needs, I need to deal with some of my "beach ball" issues first." So be it. Put the book away for future reference and go to the Lord and others, if necessary, for the help you need.

After one of my seminars, a Pastor's wife shared, "I am one of those "beach ball" ladies. I have tried to ignore my past and I have just kept sweeping it under the carpet, hoping it will go away. Not so. I have struggled in my Christian walk and I know I am not being the wife, mother, and Pastor's wife I want to be. I have resolved that after today, I am going for counselling and pursuing the healing I need." I strongly commended her for her courage and determination.

Conclusion

Remember: Change your Thoughts – Change your Life! If you feel your journey to wellness will be a long one, maybe it will but I pray that today will be the *first* day of that journey!

Life-Changing Questions to Ponder

♥ Can you list any circumstances or events in your past that are affecting your present sexual life?

♥ How do you think these past issues are having an effect on your present sexual life?

♥ Have you dealt with them or are you planning to deal with them?

♥ What are the steps you feel you must take in order to be released from your past?

♥ What is the reason(s) you are not going for help?

♥ Do you believe God can forgive you for your past?

♥ Will you forgive *yourself* for your past? Will you fully accept God's forgiveness?

The Life-Changing Word...
Memorize/Meditate

"If we confess our sins, he is faithful and just and will forgive us our sins and purify us from all unrighteousness."
I John 1:9 (NIV).

♦ ♦ ♦

"Therefore, if anyone is in Christ, he is a new creation, the old has gone, the new has come!" I Corinthians 5:17 (NIV).

♦ ♦ ♦

"Forget the former things, do not dwell on the past. See, I am doing a new thing!" Isaiah 43:18 (NIV).

♦ ♦ ♦

"Forgetting what is behind and straining toward what is ahead, I press on ..." Philippians 4:13 (NIV).

♦ ♦ ♦

"For I know the plans I have for you," declares the Lord, "plans to prosper you and not to harm you, plans to give you a hope and a future." Jeremiah 29:11 (NIV).

My Prayer to the
Life-Changer

Dear God: After reading this chapter, I...

_____

_____

_____

_____

Chapter Three

UNDERSTANDING...

How
Men
Are Wired

"Become aware of each other's
needs and learn to meet them." [1]
Willard J. Harley Jr.

Let The Women Speak:

♥ "I can't seem to change my husband; he can't get enough sex."

♥ "My husband is continually gawking at me; he checks me out around the clock."

♥ "I get frustrated with my husband when he rushes through sex. He is too quick for me."

♥ "Are you being a hypocrite if you make love even when you aren't in the mood?"

♥ "I can't be sexy – I'm no model. I've got lots of flaws."

♥ "My husband isn't interested in sex. What's the matter with me?"

"Passion, sexual desire – what's that?"

Most men have the following sexual characteristics:

- Men are greatly affected by their high testosterone levels.

- They can be aroused quickly and can climax quickly.

- They are visually stimulated.

- A man's self-esteem is connected to how well things are functioning at home – especially in bed.

(These are general tendencies and are not true in all cases)

We are not able to change the way God created our husbands. From the moment of conception, chromosomes have encoded masculine characteristics into every cell of their bodies. They are and always will be *very* different from us.

The sooner you understand that your husband is wired totally different from you and that *nothing* you can do will change that fact, the happier you will become. Instead of trying to alter or change his God-given makeup, try to accept, accommodate, and appreciate the differences.

A prayer that you may want to memorize and reflect on is:

"God grant me the serenity
to accept the things I cannot change,
The courage to change the things I can,
And the wisdom to know the difference."
(Reinhold Niebuhr)

Stop and meditate on the truth in this succinct prayer. Let's face it! Some things *we can change – some things we cannot.* The title of John Gray's book, *Men are From Mars, Women are From Venus* [2], says it all!

Many women spend an entire lifetime trying to redesign their husbands and sing this rewritten version of a familiar chorus ...

> *Change His Make-Up, O God*
> *Make it ever new*
> *Change His Make-Up, O God*
> *May he be like me*

> *I am the potter – He is the clay*
> *Mould him and make him*
> *Just like me today...*
>
> *(Adapted from Change My Heart, Oh God*
> *by Eddie Espinosa © 1987 Mercy Publishing)*

Having this attitude will result in much frustration and marital unhappiness.

Let's explore a few differences:

A̶ffected by Testosterone

The sex hormone in the male body is testosterone. It increases in production at the onset of puberty and reaches its peak levels of production in a man's early twenties. This hormone remains at a steady level within the male body until aging has some effects.

Though it is not always true, many women find some of their sexual desire is tied to a hormonal cycle. Men do not experience this phenomenon, and their testosterone, the hormone that creates desire in both men and women, creates a fairly consistent desire for sex.

As Linda Dillow and Lorraine Pintus state in *Intimate Issues,* "Hormone levels greatly influence sexual desire. A man is like a river. His testosterone levels flow constant and steady. A woman is like an ocean. Her hormones ebb and flow, depending on where she is in her menstrual cycle. In the early part of her cycle when estrogen levels are high, desire for sex can wash over her with the force of a typhoon. Several days later, after ovulation, she may want nothing to do with sex - ever again.

"A man has seventeen sexual glands. Like millions of Energizer Bunnies, these glands work day and night, producing semen, which is stored in an inner sac in the testes. When the sac fills up, his testes tells his brain, 'Do something quickly before I explode!' A man's need for sex is not all in his mind; his sexual command center demands release from the accumulated build-up." [3]

We, as women, must recognize that a man's need for sex is *not* an option – it is a biological and physiological *need*.

(Obviously, this need is superseded by the need for air, water, food etc., but this desire cannot be overlooked or minimized.)

After becoming aware of this fact, I needed to rethink and reprioritize what I perceived Simon needed from our marital relationship.

According to extensive research Dr. Willard Harley, Jr. has done, "the *first* thing men cannot do without is sexual fulfillment." [4]

*M*en Are Aroused Quickly and Climax Quickly

At all of my seminars, questionnaires are given to the participants. Ladies share what the most frustrating aspect about their sexual relationship is. Almost without exception, the response is the same: too many "quickies!", sex too quickly!

Let's describe the usual scenario: Our husbands want sex much more often than we do.

They want it quickly most of the time at least, too quickly for us. So what happens? We, as women, feel resentful, used, and angry, and our husbands feel rejected, put down, and upset. A power struggle usually ensues, with both partners feeling very unhappy and unfulfilled.

We certainly experienced all of the above in our bedroom and had to work through this common frustration. We just didn't seem to understand each other and didn't know how to solve the problem.

Because I recognize the effectiveness of using word pictures, I shared a few with Simon in the hope that he would understand my perspective.

One evening I set our crockpot on the counter beside our microwave. On the crockpot, I put a sticky note stating, "Ruth in bed - a crockpot." On the microwave, I put another note: "Simon in bed - a microwave!!" Simon roared with laughter when he read my notes, and indicated that I had stated my point directly and effectively.

Ruth - in Bed

Simon - in Bed

Another analogy I shared was that of a birthday cake sparkler and a candle. The sparkler represented Simon in bed and the candle represented me. I lit both.

I reminded him that although the sparks are wildly flying for him while we make love, he burns out in minutes, while the wax in my candle is barely melted in the same time span.

This analogy illustrates that both spouses have different needs that have to be addressed in order to ensure each other's fulfillment.

One helpful illustration we discovered in some sex manuals was a food analogy.

Sexual encounters can be thought of in three ways: as fast-food snacks, main course meals, or a smorgasbord of gourmet delights.

Fast-Food Sex – Quickies

Fast-food sex is like a mini-meal or a quick treat. Both partners agree, for whatever reasons, that a long sexual encounter is not appropriate at that time. Like snack food, "quickies" are easy to prepare, take little energy, but do not totally appease the appetite or make up the total diet.

Quick sex can occur late at night after a tiring day, or it can be a rapid rendezvous between other commitments. Quickies can be fun - a sunrise special, or a bedtime relaxer.

As Cliff and Joyce Penner say, "Quickies cannot be the sustenance of your sexual diet. You can survive on quickies, but you will not grow; you will stagnate. Continue to weave them in between your complete meals. They add spark and variety." [5]

Some days, due to weariness or simply not being in the mood, you could ask your husband if a quickie or fast-food sex would meet his immediate need for sexual release.

Because these quick sexual encounters can be completed in minutes, you might ask yourself if you can muster up three to five more minutes of energy. You can probably do that *and* with a pleasant and cooperative attitude. The end result is that your husband is happy and so are you. Since you did not turn him down, you don't feel guilty about not meeting his needs and because he didn't have to pressure you or nag you for intimacy, he is happy. This is a win-win situation.

In most cases, women will have to recognize that their husbands' needs for sex will be greater than theirs. This does not mean you have to become a cheap call-girl and jump every time your husband snaps his fingers.

No, you do not have to become a mindless robot or a love slave to him. Rather, choose to make yourself available for "quickies" at times, and do not become resentful or feel used. Your husband, in turn, has to realize that in order for you to be sexually healthy, happy and well-balanced, you need frequent main course meals.

Someone asked me, "Should you make love even when you are not in the mood?" And my answer is "Sometimes." If you are determined to make sex a priority, you do not always have to wait until you are in the mood. You can just act. It is an act of your will. Whoever told you that love is a feeling is only partially right. Love is an act of the will. If you love your husband, you can choose to meet his needs - with or without the warm fuzzy feelings.

I Corinthians 7:3 says,

> *"The husband should fulfill his marital duty to his wife, and likewise the wife to her husband. The wife's body does not belong to her alone, but also to her husband. In the same way, the husband's body does not belong to him alone but also to his wife."* (NIV).

Another verse to ponder is *"Give and it shall be given to you."* Luke 6:38 (NIV). When you choose to lovingly give the gift of your body to your husband, and to sensitively and appropriately meet his needs, you will find he may reciprocate in grand style. The more you actively pursue meeting his needs, the more he may actively pursue meeting yours.

"Don't you think it is hypocritical or phony of you to make love when you are not *really into it?*" quizzed one woman. Again, I would say "No." You do many things for your husband when you're not in the mood, simply because you know your responsibilities. For example, you might not always feel like making meals, doing the laundry, or picking up dirty underwear, but you do it regardless of how you feel - with a good attitude or with a poor attitude. It is the same with sex.

*M*ain Course Regular Meals

A well-balanced nutritional meal sexually is mutually satisfying for both partners, and it occurs when neither partner is fatigued or in a rush. These types of sexual meals are not consumed quickly; they have variety and satisfy deep hunger.

Main course sexual meals usually require planning and taking time. Most couples do their best when time is set aside to bring their worlds and bodies together, to pleasure and enjoy each other's body, and to be free to allow arousal, release, and intercourse, as desired.

John Gray, in his book *Men are From Mars, Women Are From Venus*, says that "this type of sexual encounter takes thirty minutes to build to orgasms; five minutes for him, twenty for her, and then, five minutes more to enjoy the afterglow of lying together in love." [6]

Smorgasbords – Gourmet Delights

A special occasion, like an overnight getaway, is the time to indulge in a smorgasbord of sexual delight. Long, luxurious romance, and lovemaking with no time constraints, provides a balance to fast-food sex.

Perhaps a "hers" night or "his" night would be in order. Each partner would take turns choosing favorite sexual activities while the other partner would oblige these wishes to the fullest. For example, the wife may say, "Tonight I want to pleasure you – tell me how." (See page 98 for qualifying note.)

These kinds of encounters may take a great deal of preparation with attention to such details as music, lighting, flowers, setting, appealing night wear, and intriguing props. Take turns planning these "sex-sational" encounters. By doing this, you alleviate the pressure of one spouse having to come up with creative and stimulating ideas all the time.

An ongoing diet of gourmet meals, of course, would be far too rich, but it is enjoyable once in a while.

While this analogy is a good one, we have come up with our own. Because Simon and I are both very musical, we have chosen a musical analogy.

Sometimes sex is like a jingle or commercial – quick, to the point, exciting, and captivating.

At other times, sex is like a long-playing CD – much slower, less rushed and relaxing.

And lastly, sex is sometimes like a symphony. It can be an entire evening of musical delights – a special rich and in-depth experience.

"The sexual experience is like two unique musical instruments harmonizing together, playing a beautiful song that both enjoy. The instruments are different and respond in different ways to touch and stimulation. At times one instrument takes the lead in the song, and vice versa. Both do not have to sound the high note at the same time! Both instruments seem to complement the other. So in lovemaking discover how to please each other in different ways. Let each lead from time to time. You can find wonderful harmony!" [7]

Men are Visually Stimulated

If you are married to a normal man, this is not new material.

According to Dr. Bernie Zilbergeld, author of *The New Male Sexuality*, "a man's optic nerve is directly connected to his penis." [8]

Recent stats regarding the continually growing pornography industry certainly validate this fact. Today's legal porn business is a $56 billion global industry. In 1998 Americans rented 686 million X-rated tapes, and this year's X-rated videos should generate some $5 billion in sales and rentals, doubling the revenue of five years ago. [9]

For most men, the connection between an erotic image and sexual arousal is very powerful and instantaneous. A woman can drive by a handsome male jogger, notice his muscular physique, and almost immediately forget that visual stimulus. A man can see a cute female jogger and almost drive off the road trying to see in the rearview mirror what her breasts look like. He may even fantasize further about the cute jogger as he mentally tunes in to other sexual cues. [10]

Many women are continually chiding their mates for visual interest in their bodies and seem to resent this fact.

Once again, we need to recognize that this is the way *God* made them. Men want and need visual stimulation from us, their wives. By realizing that you could provide all the visual stimulation your husband would ever need, you could suggest, "Feast your eyes, dear. What you see is what you can have!" In your private moments, you can willingly choose to present your body in a manner that really pleases him. Why feel self-conscious? You are pleasuring and pleasing your *own* husband.

Do you have to possess a perfect, flawless body? No. But what you have, use to your best advantage.

Some women perhaps feel self-conscious about their small breasts or large hips, and feel they could never be seductive with these perceived flaws. Your husband, no doubt, closely observed your physical appearance before marriage. He obviously was pleased with what he saw and hence proposed to you.

As Dr. John Gray says in *Mars and Venus in the Bedroom,* "When a man loves you, the more aroused he becomes, the more perfect your body becomes to him. The last thing on a man's mind during sex is how fat your thighs are. When a man is in love and turned on by his wife, he is also totally entranced by the feminine beauty of her body, regardless of where the media would rank it on a scale of one to ten. When he is in love with his wife, he experiences the perfection of her body for him." [11]

Don't continually beat yourself up over this matter. Make the most of what God has given you. Make the changes you feel you can to improve, and just be sexy in your own way.

What is sexy? According to Andrew Greeley, author of *Sexual Intimacy*, "to be sexy is to be aware of your body as an instrument of playfulness and delight, to be able to communicate this awareness to your husband and give him the gift of your body for pleasure, delight, variety and playfulness." [12]

Why not rejoice in the body God gave you and use it to please your husband?

According to a survey from *Psychology Today*, "one of the quickest and best ways to feel good about your body is to have a rewarding sexual relationship with your husband. Good sexual experiences breed high levels of body satisfaction." [13]

We see several examples of ladies in scripture who also recognized the power of visual appeal. Esther spent almost an entire year preparing her outward appearance for presentation before the King (Esther 1:9 &12). On the advice of her mother-in-law, Orpah, Ruth prepared her body to look physically appealing and to create interest in her prospective mate, Boaz (Ruth 3:3). The Shulamite woman, in Song of Solomon, sensuously performed an erotic dance before her lover as an invitation to lovemaking (Song of Solomon 7:1 – 3). She made herself beautiful for her husband, using her appearance to create arousal and desire in him. The vivid, detailed descriptions Solomon gives of her eyes, hair, teeth, lips, neck, and breasts make it clear that he had noticed every detail of her body and appreciated the time she had spent in preparing her body for him.

There is no shame or embarrassment in making yourself as attractive as possible for your husband. Anything that calls attention to your best features is a wonderful way to broadcast to your husband, "I'm here for pleasure and to enjoy lovemaking together." Provoking sexual desire within your husband isn't carnal – it's love. [14]

Occasionally, I have heard women object to the fact that a man is stimulated by his wife's appearance. Often women state, "If my husband really loved me, he shouldn't care what I look like or what I wear. He'll love me in any shape, form, or fashion."

I respond by saying, "I am not trying to convince you that you must be as beautiful as Cindy Crawford, nor is your worth or value tied to your physical beauty or charm. However, God made men to be visually stimulated and you should provide appealing stimulation that your husband appreciates."

According to Patricia Love and Jo Robinson in their book *Hot Monogamy*, "A thousand men were asked what turned them on the most. Of the men surveyed, 92 percent said they're most turned on by sexy lingerie. In an interesting footnote, 73 percent of these men said they relied on stimulation such as this to sustain their interest in their long-term relationship. In essence, a man who asks his partner to wear a lacy teddy to bed may be saying to her, *Please help me be monogamous.*"[15]

Most lingerie stores have alluring outfits for any size and figure. Why not delight your husband with your breasts as is recommended in Proverbs 5:19?

According to a survey conducted by the National Opinion Research Center at the University of Chicago, "the second most appealing sexual act for men and women (preceded only by intercourse) was watching a partner undress."[16] If that is true, we can easily change what we consider a mundane task into an exciting visual experience for our husbands.

Judith Newman said, "the most popular sexual activity outside actually having sex is taking showers or baths together."[17] Why not consider asking your spouse to join you more often in this daily routine? You can't lose on this proposition; you'll have lots of fun, and your husband will enjoy the visual stimulation. Your household will realize great savings on the water bill!

One lady angrily expressed after a seminar: "I'm not dressing up in these slinky outfits like some Barbie doll just for my husband to gawk at me!" My response was, "Wouldn't you rather have him looking at *you* than at some other woman at the local peep show?"

Many ladies wrongly assume that just because their husbands are Christians, they do not have the need for this visual stimulation. Some need to "wake up and smell the coffee" on this issue.

Christian or not, most men are visually stimulated. Unfortunately, many Christians are having this need met in very inappropriate forms, such as pornographic Internet sites or magazines. I have had numerous ladies that attend my seminars share the sad stories about what is transpiring in their homes.

The March 2000 edition of Dr. Dobson's *Focus on the Family Magazine* stated that "63 percent of the men who attend our *Men, Romance and Integrity* seminars admit to struggling with pornography sometime in the past year. About two-thirds of these men hold leadership positions in the church; 10 percent are pastors. Almost one in seven calls to the Focus on the Family Pastoral Care Line is about Internet pornography."[18]

I would be very careful to acknowledge that a man's addiction to pornography does not *necessarily* mean that his wife was not actively trying to provide this visual stimulation in their own home. In some cases, the wives are not being negligent in this area, but in other cases, there is a great deal of room for improvement.

I would also be careful to not stipulate that you *must* wear sexy lingerie. What I am suggesting is that you inquire of *your* husband what you could do to adequately meet *his* need for visual stimulation. (Note: these suggestions, however, *must* be mutually agreed upon and be mutually satisfying. He *must* respect your feelings and preferences. You may need to come to a compromise.) (See Chapter 6: How to Discuss Your Sexual Relationship With Your Mate.)

One lady shared that her husband wishes her to dress seductively *all* of the time – including to work and to church - and she said she felt uncomfortable appearing this way. I suggested to her that she tell her husband that she is delighted that he is pleased with her body and wants to show it off – but that she will reserve it for very private, exclusive showings, "for his eyes only." She did not want other men to enjoy what she wanted to share with him *alone*.

A Man's Self-Esteem is Connected to How Things Are Functioning at Home, Especially in Bed

A man may have great sales at work, have a great golf score, etc., but if he feels inadequate, unloved, and unappreciated by you, especially in the bedroom, he feels very depleted and unhappy.

Men want to feel that they are attractive, sexually appealing, and adored by their wives.

According to Dr. Harley in his book *His Needs, Her Needs*, admiration is one of the top five needs of a man.[19]

Solomon's wife understood a man's need for admiration. She told Solomon how handsome and charming he was and went to great lengths to describe in detail his physique.

She told him he was "outstanding among ten thousand." Most men would be happy if you told them that they were outstanding among 500!

If you take the time to read Song of Solomon, you will find that some of her words are very graphic. She made it clear that she wanted him, and was not always waiting for him to initiate sex, but made provocative advances herself.

Many men long for this type of affirmation from their wives. (Be sure to read all of the men's comments in Chapter 5.)

Men may receive many put-downs and much criticism throughout their day, but they can be soothed by our loving, caring, and affirming words inside and outside the bedroom.

One man told me, "All I want is for my wife to think I'm her number one – and she needs to verbalize that fact to me."

For most men, what makes sex fulfilling and memorable is a woman's fulfillment. They delight in the fact that they have driven her wild or taken her to higher states of ecstasy. Having a woman verbalize appreciation to him is incredibly meaningful to a man.

Many women never consider thanking their husbands for what they are doing *right* in bed, and usually only share how they could improve.

We have the power to significantly raise the self-esteem of our mates with a few sincere words of commendation. Let's do it regularly!

You're the Only One

A critical point to remember is that we, as wives, are the *only* people on this planet with the *right* and *responsibility* to meet *our* husbands' significant sexual needs.

I am not so arrogant as to believe I can meet all of Simon's needs. He has many varied social, emotional, physical, and spiritual needs. Some of these are met by the Lord, his family, friends, and colleagues.

However, when it comes to meeting this number important need, sexual fulfillment – this assignment is given to one person and one alone. ME!

"When a man chooses a wife, he promises to remain faithful to her for life. This means that he believes his wife will be his only sexual partner 'until death do us part.' He made this commitment because he trusts her to be as sexually interested in him as he is in her. He trusts her to be sexually available to him whenever he needs to make love and to meet all his sexual needs, just as she trusts him to meet her emotional needs."

"Unfortunately, in many marriages the man finds that putting his trust in this woman has turned into one of the biggest mistakes of his life. He has agreed to limit his sexual experience to a wife who is unwilling to meet that vital need. He finds himself up the proverbial creek without a paddle. If his religious or moral convictions are strong he may try to make the best of it. Some husbands tough it out, but many cannot." [20]

Conclusion

When I fully recognized that sex was an important *need* for Simon and reminded myself that I was the *only* one to meet that need, I changed my perspective on our intimate relationship. Women certainly do not want their husbands to entertain the thought of having their needs met elsewhere. By changing some of our mental "data" and in some cases reprogramming our mind, we will reap the benefits ... and our husbands would probably say the same.

What Do You Do If Your Husband "Has a Headache"?

While many women have difficulty coping with a husband who has a much greater sex drive than they do, other women struggle with the fact that their husbands do *not* desire sex.

As one can imagine, this would stir up deep feelings of insecurity, doubt, and rejection.

Some women ask themselves: "What's wrong with me? Am I that unattractive? Am I that unappealing? Where is my husband getting his needs met, if not from me?"

An expert in sexual issues made the following statement: "Ninety percent of sexual problems aren't sexual at all – they have their roots in the emotional barriers we place between ourselves and our partners. We bring these problems into the bedroom from the dinner table, the office, from our past experiences."[21]

Take time to thoughtfully consider the following questions. They may help you pinpoint the reason(s) why your husband isn't interested in sex.

- Is your husband exhausted? Over-worked? Stressed out?
- Does he have pressures at work? Has he been laid off? Fear of losing his job?
- Are you pregnant?
- Have you ever laughed at his sexual prowess?
- Have you ever become angry and verbalized harsh, caustic words with regard to his sexuality or sexual performance?
- Have you ever expressed dissatisfaction, in an unkind way, regarding how he meets your needs?
- Have you compared him to past lovers or past mates?

- Does he feel valued by you inside and outside of the bedroom?
- Does he feel confident of your love and approval?
- Have you ever initiated sexual intimacy?
- Has he stopped trying to engage in sexual activities because of your repeated rejection of his advances?
- Are his needs being met elsewhere? Internet? Pornography?
- Does he have unresolved guilt from the past?
- Are there unresolved issues between you that haven't been properly addressed?
- Have you reviewed his family history?
- Was his father distant? Unloving? Abusive?
- Does he have a reason to hate women? Was he abandoned as a child by his mother?
- Was he told by his parents that sex was sinful?
- Was he involved with premarital sex?
- Has he ever fathered a child out of wedlock?
- Has your husband been sexually abused?
- Does your husband have low self-esteem? Does he hate himself?
- Does he have any physical problems? Medical concerns?
- Is your husband on any medication?

- Does your husband suffer from impotency?

- Has your husband been unfaithful to you? Have you forgiven him and worked through this issue or does he still think you hate him for his actions?

- Are you in a rut? Is your sexual life predictable and boring?

- Are you saving enough energy for him, or is he angry with you because you rarely have time for lovemaking?

- Do you feel you are doing everything in your power to please him sexually or does he feel you really don't care?

After considering this list of questions, you may have discovered a possible reason for his actions.

So now what?

Talk to God. He knows and understands your feelings and frustrations. God wants to help you and your husband achieve the sexual pleasure and intimacy in marriage that He intended.

If you think you have identified what the problem is, then ask God for wisdom as to how to respond.

James 1:5 says, *"If you want to know what God wants you to do, ask him and he will gladly tell you, for he is always ready to give a bountiful supply of wisdom to all who ask him; he will not resent it."* (TLB).

Next, have an honest talk with your husband. Be very sensitive to his feelings and gently approach the topic with a great deal of love, understanding, and prayer.

Be prepared to obtain whatever medical and/or spiritual help your husband may require. Be willing to budget for professional counselling if that is necessary. Purchase books that you could read separately or together on his area of need.

If your husband refuses to talk about it, and you feel you must share your feelings with someone, then find a trusted friend or Christian counsellor who will give you some insight on how to respond.

During this time, guard your own eyes, heart, and activities. Some Christian women who would never look at pornographic literature or watch X-rated videos spend countless hours fantasizing while reading steamy romance novels or watching sensuous soap operas. Don't allow yourself to live in this fantasy world. Don't fall into this sexual temptation.

Also, be cautious about your behaviour around other men. Because your needs are not being met at home, the possibility of you flirting or making sexual advances to other men is greater. If you get caught in this trap, you'll intensify your problems. Stay close to the Lord during this difficult time and He will give you the strength to remain faithful and committed to your marital relationship.

What Do You Do If

You Have Lost Your Sexual Passion?

Many women have complained that they have lost their passion or desire for sex. The romantic sparks they used to experience seem to have faded into a fizzle.

Refer to the questions listed above. There may be some very justified physiological or emotional reasons why you are disinterested in sex. Take the time to honestly assess where you are at and why.

If you need counselling, prayer, or medical attention, then proactively pursue it as soon as possible. Don't wait or procrastinate. Remember, because your husband's sexual needs are not being met, you are leaving him vulnerable to great sexual temptation.

Start sharing small, loving words and actions with your husband on a consistent basis, even when you don't feel like it. Start focusing on the things about your husband that you love and that you feel he is doing right. (He can't possibly be doing everything wrong!) Verbalize those thoughts and feelings to him often, and remind yourself of these facts. Try to be positive.

Have an honest talk with your husband. Refer to some of the questions in Chapter 6. There may be unresolved issues between you that will not be rectified by "sticking your head in the sand."

Share your feelings with the Lord in prayer. He made you and knows everything about your makeup. He can give you the strength and direction to change in this area. Ask Him to increase your sexual desire and expect great answers to prayer.

Why did you feel a great deal of passion and excitement when you were dating? Probably because you were spending lots of time and energy pleasing your mate in every way possible. After marriage, you may have gotten into a rut and are now taking your husband for granted.

Romance and passion can be compared to a roaring fire. If you want to maintain a blazing fire - you must consistently add the kindling through kind words and actions. Change your actions *first* and your emotions will soon catch up! Try it – it will work for you. You can do all things through Christ, who strengthens you! (Philippians 4:13) (NIV).

Life-Changing Questions to Ponder

♥ Do you feel you have a good understanding of your husband's sexual makeup and needs?

♥ Should you consider purchasing some books to help assist you in gaining a better understanding?

♥ Have you ever prayed "Change *His* Heart, O God?" Do you need to change the words to "Change *My* Heart, O God?"

♥ Can you relate to the food-sex analogy? Will it help you understand your husband's needs better? Do you need to take time to share some creative word pictures with your husband?

♥ Are you providing the visual stimulation your husband may need and enjoy?

♥ Are you enhancing your husband's self-esteem by your loving responses to his sexual advances? Are you verbalizing your love and pleasure to him regarding his lovemaking ability?

♥ Have you accepted the fact that your husband will have different sexual characteristics from you and that there is little you can do to change that?

♥ Do you need to add some "kindling" to your sexual and romantic relationship in order to keep the passionate feelings burning? What type of kindling should you add right away?

The Life-Changing Word...
Memorize/Meditate

"Let my charms and tender embrace satisfy you
Let my love alone fill you with delight
Proverbs 5:19 (TLB adapted).

♦ ♦ ♦

"I belong to my lover and his desire is for me." (NIV).

♦ ♦ ♦

"Kiss me again and again, for your love is
sweeter than wine" Song of Solomon 1:2 (TLB).

My Prayer to the
Life-Changer

Dear God: After reading this chapter, I...

_____

_____

_____

_____

Chapter Four

UNDERSTANDING...

How The Seasons of a Marriage Affect Your Sex Life

"To everything there is a season."
Eccl.1:1 (KJV).
"Just as there are seasons in our individual lives, so are there seasons in a marriage. To know these stages of development ahead of time, is to be prepared for them."
H. Norman Wright [1]

Let the Women Speak:

- ♥ "I'm so apprehensive and uptight about my upcoming marriage and how I will respond to my sexual life with my husband!"
- ♥ "Stretch marks, sagging boobs, and a flabby stomach – is that what you call sexy?"
- ♥ "My husband doesn't seem to want sex in his old age. – What's the matter with me?"
- ♥ "I'm so tired after chasing around three preschoolers – the last thing on my mind is lovemaking. Sex is just one more chore!"
- ♥ "Counselling would help us, I'm sure – but what would people think?"
- ♥ "How do I meet all the needs of my demanding children, my demanding husband, and a demanding job?"

The Seasons of a Marriage:

    A. The Honeymoon Season

    B. The Newlywed Season

    C. The Childbearing Season

    D. The Childrearing Season

    E. The Empty Nest Season

A. The Honeymoon Season

Most girls are meticulous about planning every detail of their wedding day to ensure all of their dreams will come true; however, some put little effort into planning their honeymoon.

Yes, they have arranged for the plane tickets to their exotic and romantic destination and have a new wardrobe of clothes to take with along, but few have actually taken the time to sit down with their fiancé and discuss the sexual aspect of their honeymoon.

Failure to do this can be disastrous and can have lasting consequences. Some couples have never really recovered from the wounds or misunderstandings that occurred on their honeymoon.

While this isn't a comprehensive list, here are some things to consider if you are engaged:

1. Get to Know Yourself
2. Get to Know Your Partner
3. Read Many Sex Manuals and Guides Privately and Together
4. Discuss Your Contraceptive Alternatives
5. Talk about Expectations on your Wedding Night
6. Carefully Plan Your Honeymoon Details

1. Get to Know Yourself

A healthy and exciting sex life begins by knowing yourself, personally and sexually.

You must know who you are as a person and what you will contribute to your sexual relationship with your mate.

A few questions you may wish to ponder would be:

- What are you like? (outgoing / introverted? organized/chaotic?)
- How would you describe your personality type?

(For instance, if you would describe yourself as shy, fearful, and easily intimidated, you must endeavour to understand how these characteristics are going to affect how you relate to your mate in bed.)

- A great resource in helping you to define yourself is Dr. LaHayes' book, *Spirit Controlled Temperament*. Another helpful tool that most ministers use in their premarital counselling is the Myers Briggs Type Indicator™.

- Would you say you have a healthy self-image? What about positive self-esteem?

- Do you feel worthy of being loved? How can you really love someone else, if you dislike yourself?

- What is your sexual history?

- Have you been abused or raped, or did you engage in premarital sex?

- How was sex discussed in your home? How did your parents relate to you and to each other?

- Have you been exposed to pornography?

- Have you been married previously? What positive or negative memories will you bring with you from that sexual relationship?

- What do you think of your body? Do you like or dislike your body?

- What messages have you been given by others about your body?
  - (For instance, if your brothers teased you mercilessly about being flat-chested all your life, how do you think these comments are going to affect your relationship with your new husband?)

121

- Do you think you are attractive?
  - (The question isn't whether you think you are a perfect model with a flawless figure.) However, the way you feel about your body will affect how openly you will be able to share yourself, how freely you will allow someone else to touch and caress you, and how enthusiastically you will go after sexual pleasure for yourself.
- What illnesses, family history, or health problems have you experienced that may have an impact on your sexual life?
- Have you ever had any problems with your menstrual cycle? your breasts? any infections?
- Have you had any problems with your mental health, such as, depression? or anxiety attacks? Have these been treated or are they being treated?
- Have you ever had close intimate relationships and friendships before? Can you trust people?
- How would you define intimacy? Do you really know what your expectations are in this area?
- Do you hate or dislike men? Were your past relationships with men positive or negative?
- Have you received healing in these delicate areas?
- How would you describe your spiritual life?
  - Are you a growing, maturing Christian?
  - Are you actively seeking God's will for your life?

- Are you spiritually disciplined? (Regular Bible reading, prayer, and church attendance.) Remember – engaging in sexual intimacy does not involve merely the joining of two physical bodies. It is greatly impacted by your spiritual intimacy. The closer you are to the Lord, the closer you will become as a couple.

This list is by no means comprehensive, but it will get you started in thinking about yourself.

By getting to know yourself, you will be able to analyze the "baggage" you bring to your marriage, as well as the strengths you have. The answers to these questions will have huge implications for your sexual happiness.

If appropriate, you may wish to seek professional Christian counselling with regard to difficulties you perceive in yourself. The healthier you are as an individual - physically, emotionally, and spiritually - the better woman and lover you will be.

2. Getting to Know Your Partner

Obviously, the more you know about your fiancé's past, the more you will be able to understand him and meet his needs.

Use a list of questions similar to those above to enquire about your mate. (Also refer to Chapter 6: How to Discuss Your Sexual Relationship with Your Mate.)

Two very personal and vital questions I asked Simon *before* we got engaged were:

1. Did you or do you have a struggle with pornography? (I listed every possible form I could think of before awaiting his response.)

2. Have you ever struggled with any homosexual tendencies?

I remember the night I asked him these questions. He responded by saying, "Wow, girl! You really shoot from the hip and ask straightforward questions!" And I replied, "I simply don't want any surprises along these lines after we are married.

"DARLING, THERE'S SOMETHING YOU SHOULD KNOW ABOUT ME."

© Copyright John McPherson (Used by permission)

If there is something I need to know that will impact our marital happiness, I want to know *now*. I give you the same permission to ask similar personal and intimate questions of me. I feel you have a right to know."

The reason for my extreme caution in this area is that I have known couples who did not adequately discuss these issues or were not totally honest with each other. Consequently, they are divorced today. One gorgeous bride, eagerly anticipating a meaningful sex life, was devastated on her honeymoon when she found out that her new husband was not attracted to her in any way. He was not interested in consummating their marriage, simply because he was a homosexual.

Another woman who talked to me at one of my seminars indicated that she was totally unaware that her husband was addicted to pornography when they married. He preferred to masturbate while looking at other nude photos, rather than to make love to her. This lady has faced much pain and many problems.

One bride-to-be asked me what she should do if, after asking such questions, she found out her fiancé was addicted to pornography. My answer to her was to postpone or call off the wedding until he has received help in this area. Hiding your head in the sand and pretending this problem does not exist is ludicrous and very foolish.

Without reservation, I can affirm that just placing a wedding ring on another person's finger will not ensure that all prior concerns and problems will somehow vanish. If anything, being married only accentuates them.

Also, ask your fiancé if he was a virgin and/or if he is a father. There have been instances where a child that was fathered before a couple's recent marriage has appeared from nowhere after the wedding. The legal wrangling and child support issues that this would uncover, as well as the ensuing stresses on the marriage, would be profound.

If you have had a promiscuous sex life in your past, you do not need to provide your fiancé with a play-by-play description of your sexual relationships with others. The memories may haunt your fiancé. If these events have been confessed and forgiven, then leave them with the Lord. The issue that has to be discussed is whether these relationships have left you with the HIV virus, sexually transmitted diseases, or an inability to conceive children.

You will also note that I asked these very intimate questions of my "born-again, Bible-believing, Bible School graduate" fiancé. Often, people wrongly assume that if their husband-to-be says he is a "Christian," then they have nothing to worry about along these lines. I'm sorry to say that this simply isn't true in every case.

Take the time to really talk these issues through thoroughly and pray for the Lord's discernment and guidance in this area. Why knowingly or unknowingly allow yourself to enter into a union that you know just isn't going to work or is going to have huge hurdles to overcome? You owe it to yourself and to your partner to be totally honest, open, and vulnerable with each other regarding these important issues. If you need to seek professional help, then so be it. There is no shame in that.

Note: I am not saying that individuals with such problems or past negative experience are "untouchables" or undesirable mates and should necessarily be rejected forever. Absolutely not! All of us struggle with imperfections; however, some struggles will have an *enormous* impact on your sexual happiness. Enter your marriage with your eyes wide open. You have heard it said, "Love is blind, but marriage is sure an eye opener."

*C*hange Your Thoughts,

Change Your Life.

© *John McPherson (Used by permission)*

3. Read Sex Manuals and Guides Privately and Together

Many couples experience sexual difficulties, simply because they have not taken the time to educate themselves about their own sexual anatomy, as well as that of their partner. Failure to do this will result in a great deal of frustration, stress, and embarrassment.

Simon and I read several informative books together, so we had a very good understanding of each other's physical makeup.

Reading these types of books not only educated us as to our physical anatomy, but also about the differences in sexual response between a man and a woman. We became well versed on how our bodies would function during the arousal, plateau, orgasmic, and afterglow stages of lovemaking.

Many couples wrongly assume that they will just "know" what to do in that special moment, and then are sadly disappointed. I often use this example to illustrate my point. Just because a woman has the sexual apparatus to conceive a child, does not mean that she will know how to deliver the baby. She usually goes to her doctor, attends prenatal classes, and reads books so she will *know* how to respond appropriately at birth. It's the same with lovemaking – it is a *learned* skill.

Obviously, the actual experience will be different from reading about it in a book; however, it is important to be well versed in this area. There is nothing inappropriate about seeking outside help from medical professionals and sex therapists via books, tapes, or seminars to assist you in being totally prepared.

Simon and I often read these books aloud together. I found that this helped me become more comfortable and relaxed with verbalizing some of the words that deal with the intimate details of lovemaking.

Be sure to take a couple of these manuals with you on the honeymoon. Undoubtedly, you will want to refer to them.

Three excellent ones that include detailed diagrams and descriptions outlining the logistics of lovemaking are: *A Celebration of Sex* by Dr. Douglas Rosenau
(Thomas Nelson)

Intended for Pleasure by Dr. Ed and Gaye Wheat
(Fleming H. Revell)

The Gift of Sex by Dr. Clifford and Joyce Penner
(Word Publishing)

4. Talk About Contraceptive Options and Decide on an Appropriate Method for You

The wedding night is not the time to be arguing about whether your mate should put on a condom to avoid possible pregnancy. Many a couple who felt that pregnancy would not occur during their initial intercourse, found themselves holding a smiling baby nine months and *one* day later.

Enough said! Explore the possibilities and decide which method will work best for you - one that you are *both* comfortable with.

5. Discuss Your Expectations for the Wedding Night

While some may think such a discussion might take some of the mystique out of the first encounter, I would disagree. Simon and I discussed certain aspects regarding what we expected from that night.

After listening to some of the horror stories we had heard about shattered dreams and painful disappointments on a honeymoon, we were glad we did.

These discussions did not serve as rigid to-do lists. Rather, they allowed us to prepare to be flexible and flow with the moment, while still being aware of some of the other partner's feelings and preferences.

Beginning to openly share about these very personal issues while you are engaged will set the stage for ongoing and meaningful conversations along these lines after you are married.

6. Carefully Plan Your Honeymoon

Ladies often have some very special fantasies or dreams of what those first few days will be like with their "knight in shining armor." Sometimes, because of ineffective planning, they discover that some of their dreams have been dashed.

Some tips to consider might be:

• **Don't try to cram too many activities into those first few days.**

Let me share from experience. Simon and I were married in Ontario and had planned to go to Cape Town,

South Africa, for our honeymoon. There, I would be able to meet his family and enjoy the wonderful reception they had arranged. We also planned two stops in London, England and Paris, France.

While I would still consider going on this exciting trip, I would have made a few adjustments to our schedule.

We were married on a Saturday afternoon and after the reception, we drove to Niagara Falls, where Simon had thoughtfully booked a gorgeous room overlooking the falls. This arrangement was ideal, as the drive to our room was only about 90 minutes from the reception hall. We enjoyed a very special night "two-gether" and most of the next day before returning to my folks' home to open some gifts. I was still on my wedding "high" and didn't feel tired at all. Shortly after that, we headed to the airport for our long overseas trip.

Like most brides, I had worked with my parents, almost around the clock, preparing for the wedding of my dreams (which it was). By the time I arrived at the airport, though, the many late nights and excitement of all the festivities had caught up with me.

Having to cope with exhaustion, dealing with a huge time change, and handling the excitement of meeting most of Simon's family for the first time – all of these things proved to be a real challenge for me physically during those first few days.

Another friend shared the same feelings. She said, "I was so tired on my honeymoon that most of it is just a blur. My new husband, for obvious reasons, was keeping me up all night and I had to force myself to stay awake – not because I was bored or uninterested, but because I was simply fatigued beyond words."

In hindsight, Simon and I should have gone away alone in Ontario for two or three days so that we could spend some leisurely time just getting acquainted before we took our long trip. This time of restoration would have been desirable for both of us. I have even suggested to Simon that perhaps we should have waited several weeks or months to go on our extended honeymoon.

- **Avoid surprises.**

Try to plan activities that you both enjoyed before marriage and are familiar with.

Be sure to carefully discuss your expectations for the honeymoon. If one partner anticipates your honeymoon will consist of staying in bed and making love, while the other one thinks you are spending each day shopping and sightseeing, there are bound to be problems. Make sure you have planned activities that both partners will enjoy.

Give careful attention to all the details. Who is carrying the passports? Have you had any necessary your medical shots? Who has confirmed the honeymoon suite? What is the confirmation number of the car rental? Not attending to such details can bring a lot of extra stress and confusion on the honeymoon and you simply don't need that.

Ensure that the two of you will have lots of privacy and time alone. Simon and I spent about two weeks alone on our honeymoon and some of the time with family. Spending time with family can have its drawbacks. Being a nervous bride trying to make love with my husband in the same house as my new in-laws proved to be a great challenge for me! The squeaking bed and the accompanying sound effects had me in a nervous knot. Simon could not understand why this was a problem for me. He said, "My parents have been married for 40 years; they know what people do on their honeymoon. Relax!" Somehow, those words just didn't seem to help. One of the first things Simon had to learn about me was that I needed *complete* privacy if I was going to be a cooperative, relaxed partner.

An informative source for many tips and ideas on planning your memorable honeymoon and your new sex life is a book entitled *Getting Your Sex Life Off To a Great*

Start: A Guide for Engaged and Newlywed Couples, by Cliff and Joyce Penner. [2]

B. The Newlywed Season

Sexual Inhibitions

Depending on your personality and previous experiences, it may take a long time for you both to feel comfortable with each other's body.

"You seem shy or uptight to touch my privates," commented one man.

"To tell you the truth, I am. I feel like some gigantic hand is going to come out and slap my hand for touching your equipment," replied his new bride.

Many ladies have shared that they have experienced the same kind of feelings, and that it was difficult to give themselves permission to just "let go and enjoy." Some wives relate that they have a difficult time relaxing even though they know in their minds that they have the *perfect right* to enjoy it. Most men, however, as soon as they are legally married, find that the chains of sexual inhibition fall off in a flash and they are ready to get down to some serious lovemaking.

Physiological Problems

If, on your honeymoon or early in your marriage, you find that you are experiencing a great deal of pain or other problems engaging in intercourse, seek medical attention immediately.

Some ladies experience pain during intercourse because the openings of their bodies are extremely small. By bringing this concern to the attention a doctor, you may be able to undergo a simple, yet effective procedure to stretch your vagina so that you can experience painless sexual relations.

Refusal to attend to physiological problems that *can* be rectified might communicate some damaging, conflicting messages to your new groom. He may interpret your lack of attention to these concerns as selfishness or lack of interest in your mutual sexual happiness.

"*S*ex is perfectly natural, but *not* naturally perfect."

Sue Johanson [3]

Sex Every Hour On The Hour?

During our first year of marriage, Simon quite sincerely inquired if he was meeting my sexual needs. My reply was, "You are meeting needs I *don't even have! Exceedingly abundantly* above all I could ask or think!"

His reply was, "Well, I have waited 26 years to enjoy this and I have a lot of pent-up sexual energy."

"I have no trouble believing that, dear! I feel *all* of that energy and at times it is overwhelming!" Then I added, "Actually dear, I am very grateful that you did save this overabundance of love for me, rather than share it with many other girls before me."

After talking to scores of ladies after my seminars, I found that many of them were relieved to hear that they were not married to some sort of sexual animal or sex maniac – but rather to a very normal, red-blooded male. While sexual desire will certainly vary from male to male, it is believed that most men have an insatiable desire for lovemaking, and as I stated earlier, that is the way God made them.

Looking back, I'm glad Simon really enjoyed this new sexual expression to the fullest (even though at times I thought he had too much of a good thing). I doubt we'll ever again have as much free time without interruptions and diversions – at least, until we retire, and that's a long time away.

If you're a newlywed, why not just go with the flow? Enjoy the moments and give your husband the complete freedom to pursue this interest at this season of your marriage. Why not? You only live once.

Re-examine Your Expectations

Give yourself permission to explore your sexuality without a lot of expectations.

A wise friend told me not to be disappointed if we didn't get everything "right" during the honeymoon or even the first few years.

Give yourselves a chance to explore this area slowly and without pressure. Take lots of time to play "show and tell" and do it in unhurried time frames.

Bernie Zilbergeld says it well in *The New Male Sexuality*: "You are having good sex if you feel good about yourself and good about your partner and good about what you're doing." [4]

If you are experiencing difficulty in some area of your lovemaking, consider redefining your expectations. Why put yourself through years of apparent dissatisfaction when you can just simply change the rules or your own expectations? Doing this can put the joy back into your sexual life, and instead of it being a chore to be dreaded; it can become a pleasure again.

HOW TO STOP A BLANKET HOG

Don't be pressured by someone else's experience or what a book or magazine tells you. Be yourself. One lady at my seminar asked, "Do you have to sleep naked with your partner in order to be sexy? All of my friends think there is something wrong with me because I don't want to." I responded by asking her, "Do *you* think you have to sleep naked to be sexy? What does your husband say about it?" She replied that neither of them enjoyed sleeping without clothes, even though they had a great sex life. My response was, "Don't be pressured to live up to someone else's sexual standards or preferences. Do what you want as long as you and your husband are mutually satisfied and comfortable with what you are doing! Tell your friends kindly to mind their own business."

Allow Yourself Lots Of Time For Adjustments Outside The Bedroom

When I got married, I was in my late twenties, and had already experienced a great deal of personal freedom. I had gone to university on my own, had done a great deal of travelling, and had my own career, my own apartment, and my own car.

While I was delighted to have found my life partner, one well worth waiting for, I found the first three years to be a time of unbelievable adjustment and change.

Let me share some of the details....

I was a children's pastor at a large church (about 1,300) and Simon had been asked by our denomination to pioneer a new church (that means starting with three people – Simon, myself, and the Lord). I had always lived in large cities and was well accustomed to that. Our new posting was in a small town of about 4,000.

I had finished my Bachelor of Education degree and hoped to find a job as soon as we got married. Unfortunately, there were no openings when I applied.

My new role as a Pastor's wife was quite intimidating and at times exhausting. I had been used to being a free-wheeling, independent woman, and adjusting to a whole new set of expectations was a challenge.

Because both Simon and I had just finished our education, setting up a home was a financial stretch. Because I couldn't get a teaching job, we were living on one paycheque for quite a while. Being on a strict budget was a new experience for me, and having to make allowances for the fact that someone else had some plans for the same paycheque was a shock.

As you might imagine, there were many heated discussions as we tried to sort out our priorities, our responsibilities, our roles, our finances, etc. Now, when Simon and I attend wedding ceremonies and observe the wedding couple "glued" to each other at the height of marital excitement, we say, "Enjoy the day, my friends, as you have no idea what is in store for you in the next year or so of *adjusting*!"

Simon and I rarely argue now. That is because we have very little to argue about. We *thoroughly* covered everything in the first three years!

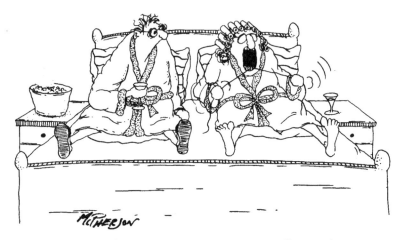

ONE OF THE 10 WARNING SIGNS THAT THE HONEYMOON IS OVER.

Due to being overloaded with change and the stress of adjustment, our sexual life was affected. If you are a newlywed, you may relate to this pressure.

One thing that really infuriated me was the fact that we could have an argument minutes or hours before bedtime and Simon seemed to be able to erase all memories of that conversation as soon as his body hit the bed. He seemed to be able to ignore the fact that we had unfinished business, and was eager get right down to the fun of lovemaking.

You can imagine the "cheery response" he got from me on those nights. Was I right? Yes and No!

"APPARENTLY I HAVE DONE SOMETHING TO UPSET YOU."

© *Copyright John McPherson (Used by permission)*

No, I don't think I should have used sex as a weapon of control, a bribe, or as a place to vent my anger. Yes, I do think it is realistic to say that what goes on *outside* the bedroom will *greatly* affect what goes on *inside* the bedroom.

In time, I learned that things did not have to be absolutely perfect in our relationship in order for us to come together physically. We had to set aside our differences and mutually acknowledge that we still had some issues to resolve.

Once we had children, this fact became even clearer to me. If my little eight-year-old son, James, came to me and wanted a hug and kiss, I would not say to him, "No way! Your room is not cleaned up, your manners are not perfect, and furthermore, yesterday you made me angry because you didn't wipe off your muddy feet." Would I say that as a mother? No, I wouldn't. I would choose to love my little boy even though he wasn't perfect and hadn't met all of my expectations. I would realize that he had lots of changing and growing up to do and that it would take many years to achieve perfection in some of these areas.

The same applied for my "big boy." Yes, we still needed to work on some areas. Both of us needed to change many things, but that didn't mean that we couldn't give each other permission to change over time and simply accept each other for what we were *at that moment*. It would be foolish to deprive ourselves of enjoying the moment. Life is too short for that kind of thinking.

Women should not manipulate men or use sex as a bribe or a reward, but frustration in the bedroom may at times reflect that there are still *big* issues that must be dealt with outside the bedroom before you can enjoy the pleasure you desire.

You may find that the harder you work on issues in the *kitchen*, the better your relationship will become inside the *bedroom*. *Continually* honing and improving your marital relationship will be well worth the effort.

Admit it, Madge. You're angry with me, aren't you?

Artist unknown

Seek Counselling

I can unashamedly admit that we pursued for counselling during these first few years. Professional Christian counsellors, trusted friends, relatives and many informative books assisted us greatly.

The Bible says, *"Listen to advice and accept instruction and in the end you will be wise."* Proverbs 19:20 (NIV). That's precisely what I purposed to do. Often I would sit, with pen in hand, listening to programs such as Focus on the Family, trying to glean information that would assist me in being a better wife.

Unfortunately, some couples interpret going to a counsellor as a sign of failure or inadequacy, or view it as a humbling or demeaning experience. Professional counsellors are paid to read books to help you answer your questions, so why shouldn't you avail yourself of their knowledge?

Other trusted friends and relatives who have already walked this path can provide invaluable tips on how to relate to your partner more effectively. Why not benefit from their wealth of experience and learn from their mistakes? Perhaps you can connect with an older couple who could serve as marriage mentors for you and your husband. They could provide the much-needed advice and counsel that you both could use.

Success in marriage consists not only in finding the right person, but being the right person.

Author Unknown

Some ladies have shared with me that their husbands will not agree to go for counselling, so I have advised them that they should go *alone*. Take responsibility for your own actions and change who you can - *yourself.* You may never be able to change your husband, but you can ask the Lord to help *you* adapt, adjust, and change wherever possible to make your marital relationship better.

C. The Child-Bearing Season

We had decided that we would wait a couple of years before we had children. Every couple will have their own schedule in this regard, but for us, this was best. Having to cope with all of the other adjustments I was having to make was enough for me to handle. Adding a crying baby would have tipped the sanity scales for me.

Very little change occurred in our sex life during my pregnancy until close to the end of my third trimester. This will be different for every couple and maybe even each pregnancy. If you experience a decrease in sexual desire, it may be because of the hormonal change that your body is experiencing. If this is the case, this needs to be lovingly shared with your spouse, as he may be unaware of your situation.

If you and your husband are having difficulty conceiving, seek medical attention. Perhaps with some minor surgery or medical counsel, you will be able to bear the children you desire. Don't let this frustration hinder or add undue stress on your sex life for long periods of time without seeking outside help.

And Then There Were Three

Simon and I were absolutely ecstatic about the arrival of our beautiful daughter Jenna. We were both very excited about being parents; we had done much reading, had taken parenting courses, and thought we were prepared for our new role. (I'm not sure one can ever be fully prepared for this role.)

Prepare For Lots Of Stress

While I knew that I would have new demands on my time, I wasn't prepared for how much stress a baby puts on a marriage. This stress was not because we were angry that we were now parents. Rather, having a baby is a stress on the mother's health, as well as on the couple's time and schedule. It really rearranges *all* aspects of their previous life.

If I could turn back the clock, I would not choose to retain all of my other commitments and simply add my mothering responsibilities. At the time, I continued all of my church work, and outside part-time work. I proceeded full-steam ahead, but with the obvious addition of a baby on my hip.

According to Audrey Edwards in *Oprah's Magazine,* "Many women are doing it all today: earning a paycheque, raising kids, putting food on the table, maintaining a home. And they are just plain exhausted – physically, mentally and emotionally. Stress saps them of any sexual feeling."[5]

Give yourself a more relaxed atmosphere in which to adapt to your new role as a mother. You may consider making the necessary financial adjustments so you don't have to seek employment outside the home, or at least not as much. Simply reduce commitments to various committees and engagements. You'll enjoy this season more. Don't try to be a *super woman*!

I probably could have handled mothering, as well as my other responsibilities, if it weren't for one thing – *lack of sleep.* I am a person who requires a minimum of eight to nine hours of quality sleep in order to function at optimum levels the next day. Neither of our babies was colicky or fussy, but both of them, for reasons still unknown to me, would wake up two or three times a night, just to visit. They wouldn't cry or scream; they would simply coo and chat and wake me up sufficiently that it was next to impossible to get back to sleep (especially when I would crawl back into bed beside a snoring husband).

© Copyright John McPherson (Used by permission)

Despite all my efforts to ensure our baby was dry, warm, and well-fed, this routine continued for the first two years of both of our children's lives. I wasn't able to sleep through a full night for about four *consecutive* years. Because of my exhaustion, the most routine, easy tasks became a struggle.

༄

ℛemember ...

Change your thoughts – Change your life!

༄

A CURE FOR SNORING

A Sex Life And Babies? Is That Possible?

After our first baby arrived, we had to wait until my body recovered from the delivery stitches, and so on. When my hormones finally stopped raging, our sex life resumed. We soon found out, however, that we had to make some adjustments to our sexual plans. Change, of course, isn't always easy. (The only person who loves change is a baby with a dirty diaper.) Transition times can be tricky and risky.

The primary stress that we had to cope with was that of my weariness. By the time I had cared for our two babies, chasing them around all day while continuing with my other responsibilities, Simon found himself into bed with a zombie! A zombie who loved him very much, but a person who, on some occasions, had very little to offer in the way of passionate lovemaking. At times, after the children had been demanding my undivided attention around the clock, the prospects of another person wanting more attention was not a cheery thought.

According to a recent article in *Oprah's Magazine* (July/Aug 2000), an estimated 24 million American women aren't interested in sex. Based on a recent study in the journal of the American Medical Association, women stated they would rather go straight to sleep.[6]

In hindsight, I would handle things differently.

Because both sets of grandparents were thousands of miles away, we didn't receive any babysitting support from them unless they were visiting. We did, however, set up a babysitting co-op at our church because there were a number of ladies with newborns. This worked very well, except for the fact that I didn't use this relief from responsibility to my best advantage. Most often when it was my turn for the free day, I would have the day planned to the minute and have 101 errands that I wanted to accomplish. While this might have been necessary occasionally, I should have at times unplugged the phone, forgot about my messy house and *slept* for the day! That would have been the most spiritual and expedient thing I could have done.

Hiring a teen to come over after school for a couple of hours to allow me to sleep could have been another option.

If you are a new mother, remember that your husband doesn't care if the house is spotless: he wants to spend time with you. You also need some quality, time alone with your husband where you feel affirmed and appreciated.

No matter how tired you are, don't give up on your love life, but do be flexible and responsive. Yes, your lives will be changed forever after children arrive, but with stubborn determination, you can find ways to stay connected. You may be thinking of waiting it out – as soon as the baby sleeps through the night, or as soon as she gets past the terrible twos. Don't count on it. In the meantime, your relationship with your mate is suffering. Do you want to spend those many years without sexual fulfillment? This is a great time for you to make a list of ways you can show love to your husband in five minutes or less.

$\mathscr{P}$lan Your Times Together

During those first days of motherhood, we didn't have frequent breaks from parenting because I had chosen to nurse our babies. I should have planned, however, to get a babysitter for a couple of hours and not dismiss the idea of a quick break with Simon. A short reprieve is better than no reprieve.

Another deterrent from going out at times was that I didn't want to spend the money. According to my calculations, an evening of entertainment, in addition to babysitting fees, was something that would strain our budget.

While being concerned with our financial stability was noble, I was erroneous in using it as an excuse for us not going away and enjoying some quality time together. If date nights become vague memories, and if your love life - sex life is placed on simmer, it will soon boil over as unattended frustration, and conflicts will arise. A word to the wise!

$\mathscr{S}$tretch Marks Are Sexy?

Another issue that was of concern to me was my "new," but not improved post-baby body. Following childbirth, I found myself unattractive. Those lovely stretch marks, the flabby tummy, and other copious deposits of fat made me want to turn the lights off and hide under the covers forever. Not a true picture of loveliness and sex appeal! One woman said, "If the truth were told, I don't exactly look or feel like a sexual being anymore – but more like a 'spit-up' rag with legs and PMS."

After I shared these feelings with Simon, he lovingly assured me that he did not have the same expectation of perfection that apparently I had for myself.

When I was done nursing our children, I took a look at myself in the mirror and was determined that I didn't want to look like that for the rest of my life.

"I'LL GIVE YOU FIVE BUCKS IF YOU'LL PUT EIGHT MILES ON THIS THING BEFORE YOUR FATHER GETS HOME."

© *Copyright John McPherson (Used by permission)*

I soon devised a fitness plan that would work for me. Aquasizing daily, powerwalks, and monitoring my diet for several months helped me regain my old form and figure. I also recognized the personal benefit of being healthy and fit and caring for my own well-being.

Inward beauty is much more desirable than outward beauty; however, I don't think we should neglect our outward appearance and appear dowdy or unkempt.

Man looks at the outward appearance and God looks at the heart (I Samuel 16:7) – but remember man *does* look at the outward.

"My definition of beauty is doing the best with what you have to work with! We are not all cover girls who possess perfect model-type bodies, but I think we can all work to accentuate our positives and diminish our negatives. Regular exercise, in whatever form is most enjoyed, a good balanced diet, and up-to-date hair and clothing styles go a long way toward making us the beautiful ladies we are capable of being," shared one woman.

D. The Child-Rearing Season

After a few years, our children were off to school and we entered another era. I was enjoying complete nights of sleep, and school forced all of us into a very predictable routine.

Then we started into the "Mom's taxi routine" that included piano lessons, swimming lessons, soccer practices, and drama club. Because the children were at school all day, I was able to pursue other interests that had been postponed during their preschooler days.

Simon was busy pastoring a growing congregation and was really enjoying all of his commitments in this area.

One night we were watching a talk show and the speaker interviewed a man who said, "A lot of people in America suffer from a disease called TTNS." We both pricked up our ears and asked, "What's TTNS?"

He said it was a disease called **T**OO **T**IRED, **N**O **S**EX. Simon and I both laughed and agreed we suffered from this disease from time to time.

At times, I felt I had put the children's needs before Simon, and at times, he had put his career in ahead of our relationship. This is an area that I think most couples struggle with. While our children and careers deserve our best, they don't deserve our all. Simon and I have continually battled to keep all of these areas in sync and balance – and that is not an easy task.

The *best* gift you can give your children is to love your mate. If your children see a strong and growing marriage, it will significantly enhance their stability and security.

Although sometimes our kids tease us when we hug and kiss in front of them (appropriately, of course), we continually remind them that we are deeply in love and that is a huge advantage to them.

As we model loving behaviour to our mates, our children pick up on this and it provides a positive model for their own marriages. Simon has been very thoughtful in bringing me flowers from time to time. Since our son James was small, he has mimicked his father and brought me bouquets of dandelions, daisies, and other special flowers, saying, "I'm being just like Daddy."

Because children can be so demanding during these stages, you may have to establish some ground rules in order to make sure you get uninterrupted, quality couple time on a daily basis.

Often, Simon and I go and lie down on our bed to have a short chat after supper. Our children know this is our sharing time and that they shouldn't disturb us unless it is an emergency. A bathroom lock on your bedroom door will also help in this area.

We need to remember that our attitudes and actions will greatly affect our children's future, just as our parent's behaviour affected ours. It has required much planning and diligence to regularly spend the quality time we want together. Becoming parents should not make you celibate! We never *found* time – we had to *make* time.

"I'LL BE THERE IN A SECOND, DEAR. I'M TUCKING THE KIDS IN."

© *Copyright John McPherson. (Used by permission)*

My friends have told me that when their children were adolescents, they had more couple time together simply because their teens are away doing various activities with their friends, especially on weekends.

Others have shared it is increasingly difficult to have regular intimate moments, as their teenage or young adult children go to bed after they do. Again, planning ahead will be the key to maintaining your closeness during this season.

E. The Empty Nest Season

Obviously, I have not reached this season yet, but allow me to share some insightful comments of ladies who have been or are at this stage:

"Don't get lazy during this time. Because there isn't the obvious pressure to conceive children and because you may not feel like your old attractive, sexy self, couples in this stage often spend little time lovemaking or being romantic. It is not necessarily a reflection that they don't love each other, but rather a reflection of taking each other for granted and simply not putting any effort into this area of their marriage. This kind of complacency is to be avoided at all costs."

"Just because my sexual drive has greatly diminished, I must always keep in mind that my husband's has varied very little. He still seems to have the same interest in our sexual relationship as he did when we were newlyweds. I cannot ignore this fact and must actively seek to meet his needs."

"I could never figure out how some couples who had lived together for 25 years would suddenly get a divorce. Now that I am at that stage, I can understand why. Much of my energy over the last several years has been diverted toward our children and their needs, and most of my husband's attention has been given to a growing business. I found that when suddenly the only person to talk to across the table was my husband, I realized that because we had neglected our special times together, we were next to strangers. I decided I must work very hard at re-establishing our marital and intimate closeness. Often men at this time are experiencing some sort of mid-life crisis and if their needs are not being met at home, they could be tempted to look elsewhere."

"Our society worships youth and it is not uncommon to hear the notion that sexual activity among us seniors is suspect or even strange. Not so! The old can do anything the young can do – it just takes them longer. We need to be patient with each other and not necessarily expect 'Olympic-type performance'. Rather, we should accommodate the changes in our bodies. We've hurried all our lives; it's now time to slow down and enjoy the moments."

One lady who attended one of my seminars had been married for over 50 years. She told me that a lot of her friends laughed at her for choosing to attend. She said, "I told them point-blank – you are never too old to learn. I want to find some new ideas to affirm my husband sexually, and I'm not letting the young couples have all the fun!!" (With a wonderful attitude like that, I'm sure her husband is a contented and happy man.)

"Use it or lose it. If we, as seniors, fail to use our sexual apparatus, it will not respond as we want. Just as exercise helps promote muscle tone, strength, and flexibility, so does regular usage of our lovemaking body parts. We've chosen to use it regularly – we're not pushing up daisies yet!"

"Be aware that many outside factors can affect your sex life. For instance, when my husband retired he suffered from low self-esteem and depression for months, which certainly affected his performance in the bedroom. His change in performance had nothing to do with his enduring love for me; rather, he was dealing with this other stress and readjustment period. Ladies need to be aware of this."

"My husband and I are enjoying our freedom – freedom from fear of pregnancy and freedom from kids! We can run around the house naked and we don't have an audience! What fun! We've waited a long time for this stage!"

"We enjoy lovemaking at any time of the day, as we are not tied to a rigid schedule. Instead of always making love at night when we were tired, like in our younger days, we make love in the morning while we are full of energy and vigor!"

"Unfortunately, my husband's poor health has contributed to our lack of a sex life. His diabetes and high blood pressure have been ongoing problems. The medication used to control and reduce blood pressure can have a serious impact on a man's potency. I have had to be sensitive to these medical problems; however, there are many other ways we can show love – sexual intercourse is not the only way. We have learned to be creative. We have also taken time to talk to each other about these changes in our bodies. This eliminates any hidden fears or stresses."

"Keep your sense of humor! We laugh a lot. Often when we get into the lovemaking act, the grunts we hear are not always expressions of love, but rather groans over body parts that don't work the way they used to. We enjoy many good chuckles together."

"I continue to buy sexy lingerie. Even though my husband needs to put on his glasses to enjoy the view, he still loves it. There are many styles and outfits that still look alluring even on an old grandma! Just like a good wine, I tell him I'm aged to perfection!"

"Menopause hit me like a ton of bricks. My mood swings, hot flashes, and general irritability did not make me a very exciting sex partner. My hormones were fluctuating and so were my feelings about myself. I felt insecure, depressed and useless at times. It was a difficult time for us. I'm glad I had an understanding husband."

"SO YOU FOUND A GRAY HAIR. BIG DEAL!"

"My husband has suffered from prostate cancer and has had the accompanying surgery. Because that had implications for our lovemaking, we simply made a decision to change our expectations. No guilt trips, no put-downs – let's just go with the flow. We agreed that we wouldn't be pressured by other's expectations about what was 'supposed' to happen. I also assured him that sex was much more than firmness of erections or vigorous thrusting."

"We enjoy sitting in our hot tub and delight in lots of cuddles and caresses as well as lots of kind, encouraging words."

"I have back problems. We have experimented with different lovemaking positions to accommodate this.

Where there is a will, there is a way! Be flexible – try new things."

"After attending one of your seminars, I went home and put the chocolate bar 'Mr. Big™' on my husband's pillow. Old Grandpa can't wipe the smile off his face and was delighted with my creative affirmation. I would say, don't let romance die. Keep doing the little things that keep the 'fire' burning. There may be 'snow on the roof', but that doesn't mean the fire can't be burning within."

"I took a seminar on how menopause would affect my body. Knowing that I would be experiencing vaginal dryness and a depletion of estrogen helped me to make the necessary adjustment in our bedroom, including using a lubricant such as K-Y Jelly™. I think many women are not well-informed about these very natural changes that will occur at this age. They then incorrectly assume that there is something wrong with them, rather than realizing it's nature having its way."

"I told my husband I need lots of gentle massaging to soothe all my aches and pains. He has become a "Master Massager" which has led to many special intimate moments together. He also applies all kinds of fragrant lotions. I really enjoy that and so does he."

In summary, being aware of the natural changes that will take place in your body during this time, as well as having a sensitivity to the feelings and needs of your mate, will ensure that the sex life you enjoyed in your younger years can be a reality in your fifties, sixties, and seventies. Your attitude toward your sexuality is the key. I really like what one of these ladies said: "Don't let the young ones have all the fun!" Again ....change your thoughts, change your life!

Conclusion

Having a clear understanding of what season you are in and the resulting implications for your sexual and romantic life, will assist you in coping with the stresses and pleasures of each new phase. Enjoy each moment. Don't rush through a season of your marriage – you'll only pass that way once.

Life-Changing Questions to Ponder

♥ What season are you and your husband presently experiencing?

♥ Can you list ways you think this season of marriage has had an effect on your sexual life?

♥ Do you need to make some realistic adjustments to your 'sex-pectations' during this season?

♥ Do you need to consider counselling or reading some informative books to help you cope with the challenges of this stage?

The Life-Changing Word...
Memorize/Meditate

"To everything there is a season...." (KJV).

♦ ♦ ♦

"I can do all things (required in this season) through Christ who strengthens men" Philippians 4:19 (NIV).

My Prayer to the Life-Changer

Dear God: After reading this chapter, I...

_____

_____

_____

_____

Chapter Five

How Men Feel

UNDERSTANDING...

"When a good man speaks, he is worth listening to."
Proverbs 10:20 (TLB).

Let The Men Speak:

The following question was asked of several hundred gentlemen: If you could share with your wife one or two things that you think would improve your sex life, what would they be?

Let's let them speak for themselves...

"Sex is like church - it doesn't mean much if it only happens at Easter and Christmas."

♦ ♦ ♦

"Showing up for sex and going through the motions is not enough. For sex to be really fulfilling, there needs to be passion."

♦ ♦ ♦

"Sex should be a fun thing; it doesn't need to be so serious. You don't have to focus to the point of having a headache – just laugh and have fun!"

♦ ♦ ♦

"Please be open and honest about the things you would like me to do for you in bed. You say you like it all, but you must have some favourites."

"Please be more proactive. Don't always make me feel like I am the only one interested in sex. Please initiate it at least once in a while!"

♦ ♦ ♦

"Please be more spontaneous. Everything does not have to be perfect – just go with the excitement of the moment."

♦ ♦ ♦

"Realize men turn on fast. Prepare!"

♦ ♦ ♦

"Don't wear flannelette; those floor-to-ceiling nightgowns don't do a thing for me."

♦ ♦ ♦

"Don't fear adventure. Let's not do the same old routine. Let's be more creative."

♦ ♦ ♦

"Lose some weight! You don't look anything like the beautiful woman I married. You have let yourself go. You do not have any medical problems; you have just not disciplined your eating and exercise habits, and unfortunately I have to suffer the consequences."

♦ ♦ ♦

"Think better of yourself – you are too hard on yourself. Your body does not have to be perfect!"

"My wife is a clean freak. She insists on keeping our home in a state of perfection. Because of this compulsion, she stresses herself out to the limit and often makes our home a tense place. While I really appreciate living in a neat and tidy house, I would be much happier if she would save some of this energy she uses on keeping the house perfect, and would have some energy for me – not just for sex – but for just having fun and enjoying each other's company. I would even gladly pay a part-time housekeeper to help her out. I care about her – not a perfect house!"

♦ ♦ ♦

"Please flirt with me like you used to do when we were dating. You don't seem to be excited to be around me – not just in bed, but most of the time. I feel like you take me for granted."

♦ ♦ ♦

"I am afraid of rejection in bed – it happens too often. Tell me what I can do to make you feel good; I'm obviously doing something wrong."

♦ ♦ ♦

"Don't be so busy. I hate coming home from work to little notes stating where you are and when you will be home. You are over-committed to various committees – they are all worthwhile, but what about saving some time for me?"

"I would like her to make comments and help while sex is happening; it means nothing if she keeps her comments until breakfast tomorrow. Talk to me."

♦ ♦ ♦

"Kids are here for twenty years, but I am with you for at least another 35 years after they leave. So pay attention to me now, because in twenty years it will be too late."

♦ ♦ ♦

"I feel helpless. When I know my wife is going to turn me down, there's nothing I can do. That's an awful feeling."

♦ ♦ ♦

"I truly desire my wife. I would like her to desire me. Is that too much to ask?"

♦ ♦ ♦

"When my wife shows no interest in sex, I feel empty, sad, discounted, left out, separated."

♦ ♦ ♦

"My wife has too many demands. She'll make time for me sexually if...the room is warm enough, it's early enough in the evening, the dishes are washed, all of the kids' needs are taken care of, she's finished all her work from the office, the dog has been taken for a walk. By the time all of these conditions are met, I'm simply not interested."

"I feel trapped. I married this woman expecting to have all of my sexual needs met by her and her alone. I am a Christian and have no intentions of fooling around on her, but after years of sexual unfulfillment, I have to admit the thought has crossed my mind."

◆ ◆ ◆

"Please loosen up and let go of prior inhibitions."

◆ ◆ ◆

"Don't assume I can read your thoughts. Don't assume that something I said once is still how I feel."

◆ ◆ ◆

"She needs to learn that she is not the only one who needs to be reassured. I am a very important part of the relationship."

◆ ◆ ◆

"It would be nice for her to make love to me instead of me being the one that is required to do 'it' to her."

◆ ◆ ◆

"Please take more interest in yourself, I still love you deeply, but I have to admit I am embarrassed with the way you keep yourself and sometimes even hesitate to introduce you with pride as I really want to. Could you please work on this? Not just for me, but for yourself."

◆ ◆ ◆

"I would like it if my partner would be more assertive and vocal about what her sexual needs are – then we would have a better relationship. A lot of my sense of value in my marriage comes from being able to satisfy my wife sexually."

◆ ◆ ◆

"I wish my wife would be less forceful and pushy in our personal dealings. This trait serves her well in her business relationships, but can lead to strained feelings when applied around the house and in bed."

◆ ◆ ◆

"I want my wife to tell me when things are bothering her. Talk to me!"

◆ ◆ ◆

"I would like my partner to be a little more confident about herself and take my compliments more seriously."

◆ ◆ ◆

"Please accept yourself – try not to change to always please others. You only have to please me, and you do!"

◆ ◆ ◆

"Don't worry so much about your job. You are very dedicated and work very hard, but it leaves you exhausted and stressed."

◆ ◆ ◆

"I would like a partner who honors me and holds me in high esteem – not one who only focuses on the things she doesn't like about me."

♦ ♦ ♦

"I wish my partner would figure out what she wants/needs exactly. You can't have something if you don't know what you want."

♦ ♦ ♦

"I wish my wife wouldn't make assumptions about me or what I am thinking or how I am. I wish she would give me credit for the things I have done."

♦ ♦ ♦

"Please communicate more. Be more independent when we are apart and be more interdependent when we are together, but never be anything less than your own person."

♦ ♦ ♦

"I wish she would write me more explicit love letters and not appear ambivalent about me."

♦ ♦ ♦

"I wish she wouldn't be so connected with her parents and her family. I often feel left out."

♦ ♦ ♦

"Don't leave all the romantic decisions up to me. Take some initiative sometimes and be creative."

"I know you were repeatedly sexually abused by your father as a child. I feel really bad about this and it has really affected you. However, I am the one who has suffered the consequences. Please go and get some professional help in dealing with the past. Our sexual life has been greatly inhibited and almost non-existent at times because of your past. Is this fair to me? Go and get help. I'll support you through it."

◆ ◆ ◆

"Spend more time talking and developing interests of your own; don't be so dependent on me for everything."

◆ ◆ ◆

"Just take more time for us away from the kids so we could rekindle our love for each other. The focus and center of the family needs to be us and how we treat and feel about one another."

◆ ◆ ◆

"Be on time! Every time I want to take her on a romantic date (i.e., dinner, concert, etc.), she is so late and behind schedule that I end up getting mad and it ruins that whole evening. She is chronically late and makes me feel like time with me is not important."

◆ ◆ ◆

"I wish she would appreciate my career despite my income and would acknowledge the things I do well for her."

"Think of sex as a sharing experience, not a giving experience."

♦ ♦ ♦

"Please surprise me once in a while – make the first move."

♦ ♦ ♦

"I wish she would be more aggressive in expressing herself – her feelings and desires, both positively and negatively."

♦ ♦ ♦

"Remember, practice makes perfect – let's keep practicing."

♦ ♦ ♦

"It would be wonderful for her to initiate sex and for it to be more of a visual experience instead of under the covers in the dark."

♦ ♦ ♦

"She usually wants to have sex when I am exhausted, late in the evening – not a good time for me."

♦ ♦ ♦

"Stop trying to change everything about me!"

♦ ♦ ♦

"Display some affection in public."

♦ ♦ ♦

"Be more responsive to suggestions!"

"Let yourself go with the flow. Be willing to explore other ways to express love."

♦ ♦ ♦

"I bought that lingerie for a reason...."

♦ ♦ ♦

"Stop talking so much."

♦ ♦ ♦

"In 38 years of marriage, my wife has not seduced me once. To have sex two nights in a row would be a real treat!"

♦ ♦ ♦

"It would be nice to see my wife naked at least once a year. I am your husband – why are you so afraid to let me see you?"

♦ ♦ ♦

"I wish you weren't so tired all the time, but this is not your problem alone. WE have created this harried lifestyle. We have chosen to over-commit ourselves financially, which means you have to work. WE need to rethink our priorities. You are simply overextended – running a home, a full-time job, church involvements. This is OUR problem that WE have to fix."

♦ ♦ ♦

Life-Changing Questions to Ponder

♥ Could any of these responses have reflected the feelings of your husband?

♥ Were there any responses that you took offense to? If yes, why do you think that is so?

♥ Would you consider sharing the comments of these men and asking your husband face-to-face which ones would reflect his feelings?

♥ Which of these comments will help you to respond to your husband's needs more effectively?

The Life-Changing Word...
Memorize/Meditate

"A married woman looks for how she can please her husband ..." I Corinthians 7:34 (NIV).

♦ ♦ ♦

"If you profit from constructive criticism, you will be elected to the wise (wo)men's hall of fame. But to reject criticism is to harm yourself and your best interests."
Proverbs 15:31-32 (TLB adapted).

Let The Men Continue To Speak ...

What things does your wife do to make you feel affirmed inside and outside the bedroom? Can you recall a special memory?

"I love her joy when we meet!"

♦ ♦ ♦

"She supports my work, is honest and trustworthy and she tells me her secrets."

♦ ♦ ♦

"She publicly supports me."

♦ ♦ ♦

"Encourages me when I am discouraged."

♦ ♦ ♦

"I appreciate all the little things she does for me throughout the day."

♦ ♦ ♦

"Planning my needs before hers."

♦ ♦ ♦

"My wife was always very self-conscious about her body. She shied away from buying revealing negligees, but one night she surprised me by wearing something

181

very appealing. For me, it was special because I knew she did it to please me and, of course, it did! She's now not afraid to wear all sorts of sexy things for me, which I really appreciate!"

◆ ◆ ◆

"Holding me – I need her hugs and cuddles after a long, stressful day."

◆ ◆ ◆

"Caring words and dinners."

◆ ◆ ◆

"Made me a surprise birthday party."

◆ ◆ ◆

"She listens to me when I need to talk."

◆ ◆ ◆

"She loves to hold my hand."

◆ ◆ ◆

"She supports my dreams when her family criticizes them."

◆ ◆ ◆

"She is very comfortable with her body. She likes to be caressed in our house/car. Doesn't mind going topless – what a way to be greeted at the door! WOW!"

◆ ◆ ◆

"I love when she plans to be intimate with me and I respect her love for our children."

"She made love to me in the car on the side of a very lonely road. She left her comfort zone to please me."

◆ ◆ ◆

"She attended a football season with me and showed real interest in it, which was very appealing to me."

◆ ◆ ◆

"When she cooks my favorite meal – roast beef and mashed potatoes – I know that we are in for a nice evening together."

◆ ◆ ◆

"She is really good to my family and takes care of them, and that means a lot to me and shows her love for me."

◆ ◆ ◆

"She is an incredible flirt and only flirts with me, but I find it to be a real turn-on!"

◆ ◆ ◆

"My wife is very creative and is always surprising me. The latest was when she had a picture taken of herself with a Polaroid camera and put it on my briefcase in the morning. She was wearing a very revealing outfit and attached a note that she would meet me at a downtown hotel for the weekend. It was a real fun and exciting day!"

◆ ◆ ◆

"She has this Bathsheba and Seven Veils dance that she does that I enjoy."

♦ ♦ ♦

"She has a really nice way of massaging my back and things always go on from there."

♦ ♦ ♦

"When I walk into our bedroom and the candle on the dresser is lit, I know she is in the mood."

♦ ♦ ♦

"By saying 'I love you' and giving me a hug and kiss when I come home."

♦ ♦ ♦

"She always looks and smells good."

♦ ♦ ♦

"She really takes care of herself – I am proud of her!"

♦ ♦ ♦

"I remember that my lover once surprised me with a weekend trip to a health spa. She never told me where we were going. She told me to keep the weekend open and picked me up from work with everything we needed.

♦ ♦ ♦

"Whenever SHE seduces me!"

♦ ♦ ♦

"When she gives up others things to be with me just because she wants to."

"Planning our future together."

♦ ♦ ♦

"Occasionally, after we make love, she tells me that she feels very lucky, that I am really something else. This makes me feel great, feeds my male ego."

♦ ♦ ♦

"She tells me how wonderful I am when I do something nice for her."

♦ ♦ ♦

"She makes me laugh. She makes me feel special. I love how she looks and how she looks at me."

♦ ♦ ♦

"Whenever I feel like the world is falling apart, she lifts my spirits!"

♦ ♦ ♦

"When she lets me know I satisfy her sexual needs."

♦ ♦ ♦

"Gifts for no reason."

♦ ♦ ♦

"For our fifth anniversary, my wife 'kidnapped' me. She arranged a weekend at a bed and breakfast place."

♦ ♦ ♦

"Complimenting me to her friends when I am not around."

♦ ♦ ♦

"The most wonderful welcome-home card when I was away. When she wrote a song about being together. It made me feel trusted."

◆ ◆ ◆

"She complimented me in ways that helped build my self-confidence and emphasized that I could relax and be me and she would enjoy whatever happened without pretense."

◆ ◆ ◆

"She listens to me and shares my feelings and beliefs."

◆ ◆ ◆

"Gave me a full- body massage once."

◆ ◆ ◆

"Going places together ON TIME!"

◆ ◆ ◆

"Never makes fun of me in public."

◆ ◆ ◆

"Dressing in nothing but a Santa Claus hat and waiting under the Christmas tree when I arrived home from the office."

◆ ◆ ◆

"She compliments me to her friends. I love overhearing those conversations."

◆ ◆ ◆

"I love her conversation and imagination."

"She's always there when I need her. I like hands-on affection."

♦ ♦ ♦

"Breakfast in bed on the weekend."

♦ ♦ ♦

"Pat on the butt – saying I love you."

♦ ♦ ♦

"Constant encouragement."

♦ ♦ ♦

"My wife seems totally relaxed around me, with or without clothes on. – She seems at ease with me. I like that; it puts me at ease."

♦ ♦ ♦

"I like when she really tries to please me sexually. I occasionally ask her to do things out of her comfort zone and she is willing to try at least once. – I really like that about her – a risk-taker."

♦ ♦ ♦

"She makes me feel like I am a priority in her life. I feel she puts others' needs after mine. That makes me feel so special."

♦ ♦ ♦

"She always defends me in front of her family; she speaks so well of me to them. She makes me feel confident around them."

"She somehow has maintained some of the romantic passion that we had during our courting years... she doesn't seem bored with me and I think I can still make her heart skip a beat. I love that!"

♦ ♦ ♦

"I feel that I don't have to earn her love. She makes me feel confident that even when I do some stupid, thoughtless, and at times even rude things to her, I know she still loves me and that we can fix things together."

♦ ♦ ♦

"I love when she gives me this sexy smile and wink from the other side of the room. She knows how to catch my eye."

♦ ♦ ♦

"My wife allows me to cry in her arms ... and she doesn't make me feel like I am some sort of wimp. I feel I can become totally undone in her presence and she doesn't make me feel bad about it. I was never allowed to express negative feelings in the home I was brought up in. She is also equally good at allowing me to let off some hot 'steam' when I am frustrated at work or at home and she doesn't scold me or seem fazed by it."

♦ ♦ ♦

"I love when she dresses to please me. I think she really values my opinion and allows me to be really honest."

♦ ♦ ♦

"I remember when she went all out in looking her best for a company party we attended. I was so proud to introduce this beautiful looking lady as MY wife. I appreciate the effort she made and continues to make."

♦ ♦ ♦

"My wife has made an effort to enjoy the things I enjoy. She has learned how to fish just to please me. This allows us to spend lots of quiet moments together in a boat, fishing and ...."

♦ ♦ ♦

"My wife keeps me organized; she helps me remember all the family birthdays, helps me pick out presents."

♦ ♦ ♦

"I like the way my wife expresses gratitude for all the little things I do around the house. She doesn't take me for granted."

♦ ♦ ♦

"Her constant prayers for me - she constantly supports me in this way."

Life-Changing Questions to Ponder

♥ Did you find that there were recurring messages that the men expressed?

♥ Did you gain any ideas that you might want to try with your husband?

♥ Which of these responses may have reflected the feelings of your husband?

The Life-Changing Word...
Memorize/Meditate

> *"Be quick to listen, slow to speak, slow to anger."*
> James 1:9 (NIV).
> ♦ ♦ ♦
> *"A fool thinks she needs no advice,*
> *but a wise woman listens to others."*
> Proverbs 12:15 (TLB - adapted).

My Prayer to the
Life-Changer

Dear God: After reading this chapter, I...

_____

_____

_____

_____

PART TWO

Two-Gether Intimately ...

Meeting Your Husband's Sexual Needs

MEETING...

Chapter 6   How to Discuss Your Sexual
             Relationship with Your Mate

Chapter 7   How to Plan Your Sex Life

Chapter 8   How to Make Romance a Part of
             Every Day

Chapter Six

MEETING...

How to Discuss Your Sexual Relationship with Your Mate

Your ability to talk openly and with total honesty about your intimate relationship is key to a passionate, growing sex life.

Let The Women Speak:

- ♥ "We never talk about sex."
- ♥ "That topic is taboo at our house."
- ♥ "I don't know how to start a conversation on the topic. I'm too embarrassed."
- ♥ "My husband keeps everything bottled up."
- ♥ "I have trouble verbalizing my feelings."
- ♥ "My husband is not interested or too busy. He says I talk too much. He never listens!"
- ♥ "We have not had a good discussion about sex since our premarital counselling."
- ♥ "I'm afraid of his reaction if we talk about sex – either he'll get mad or he'll feel hurt. I just leave it alone."

Why Is It So Difficult For Couples To Talk About Their Sexual Needs And Desires?

Considering the mindset of our present society, it seems that couples should be able to talk freely about sex – especially in the context of a Christian, committed, loving relationship.

It seems odd that two individuals who have been sharing their bodies in the most intimate way possible, may not have been able to talk about the most basic aspects of their sexuality. Communication in marriage is like blood to our body – we can't live without it.

Why Don't We Talk About Sex?

A number of important studies have underscored the importance of being able to talk openly about sex. In one study, women who were able to talk openly about their sexual needs indicated they had sex more often and were more orgasmic than women who were verbally inhibited. A *Redbook* magazine survey of more than one hundred thousand married women determined that the strongest indicator of sexual and marital satisfaction among the women was "the ability to express sexual feelings to their husbands." The more they talked, the better they rated their sex lives, their marriages, and their overall happiness.

As is evident from the following table, 56 percent of the women who "always" discussed sex rated their sex lives as very good. Only 9 percent of the women who "never" talked about sex had enjoyable sex lives.

Wives Who Discuss Sex With Their Husbands				
Women	Always Discuss sex	Often Discuss sex	Occasionally discuss sex	Never discuss sex
Percentage in each category who rated sex life as very good.	56%	43%	21%	9%

"Talking about sex doesn't 'destroy the magic' – it may make the magic come alive." [1]

Sometimes, however, it will take time to get to the "magic," and it often requires sheer determination to understand your mate's feelings and thoughts.

Communication Considerations In Marriage

If you are like most couples, you have married someone who is quite opposite to you. You chose this person because your mate was different from you and that is what attracted you to him. (How is it that some of the very qualities that attracted you to your spouse now seem to be a source of irritation?)

Recognize That Your Spouse Probably Has A Different Communication Style.

Take a moment to do the following questionnaire with your mate. It will assist you in identifying your communication styles.

Circle <u>your</u> answers.

Put an X through your <u>spouse's</u> answers.

Never	Rarely	Sometimes	Often
1	2	3	4

I am talkative.
1   2   3   4

I like to talk about issues early in the morning. Don't talk to me after 10 pm. My brain has shut down.
1   2   3   4

I like to talk about issues late at night.
1   2   3   4

Never	Rarely	Sometimes	Often
1	2	3	4

I pay attention to the body language of others – visual details.
1   2   3   4

I give short, concise answers to most questions.
1   2   3   4

I can verbally express my thoughts in an organized fashion.
1   2   3   4

I don't mind speaking in front of crowds and am not intimidated by them.
1   2   3   4

I am a private person; I keep most of my thoughts to myself.
1   2   3   4

It is easy for me to identify my feelings. I am in touch with my feelings.
1   2   3   4

I only let people know what I want them to know about me.
1   2   3   4

I have difficulty trusting that people will keep confidences.
1   2   3   4

I believe that people are not really interested in my thoughts.
1   2   3   4

Never	Rarely	Sometimes	Often
1	2	3	4

I have difficulty verbally stating my thoughts in private and public.
1 2 3 4

I have difficulty defending my thoughts verbally.
1 2 3 4

I have difficulty expressing my feelings.
1 2 3 4

I base my decisions more on logic than emotions.
1 2 3 4

I don't like to talk about intimate things.
1 2 3 4

I like to keep my distance from people and their lives.
1 2 3 4

I love to have lengthy conversations with people.
1 2 3 4

"*THAT'S ONE OF THE THINGS I LOVE MOST ABOUT NORMAN. HE'S A TERRIFIC LISTENER.*"

© *John McPherson (Used by permission)*

Never	Rarely	Sometimes	Often
1	2	3	4

I can engage in small talk for long periods of time.
1 2 3 4

I feel overwhelmed when people jump from one thought to another.
1 2 3 4

I talk fast.
1 2 3 4

I speak slowly, often pausing to think.
1 2 3 4

I often finish the sentence of the person who is talking.
1 2 3 4

I often interrupt the person I am talking to.
1 2 3 4

I dislike small talk and always want to get to the bottom line.
1 2 3 4

I am very emotional and often cry when I am telling a story.
1 2 3 4

I am a detail person. I want to know exactly what happened, when, why, and how.
1 2 3 4

I have no interest in the details; just give me a summary of the information.
1 2 3 4

Never	Rarely	Sometimes	Often
1	2	3	4

I am a visual person; I need to see issues on paper to help me clarify them.
1   2   3   4

I enjoy word pictures or analogies. They help me understand meaning.
1   2   3   4

I don't like it when a person gets emotional (i.e. cries or gets angry) when sharing on a topic; it makes me lose my focus.
1   2   3   4

I can't deal with issues as soon as I get home from work. I need some space to relax, rejuvenate. [2]
1   2   3   4

After completing this questionnaire with your mate, did it reveal some startling conclusions or did it only validate what you already knew? Take time now to make a list of your conclusions about your spouse's communication preferences.

For example, my husband:

1. prefers talking late at night – so I will try to avoid morning conversations.

2. prefers dealing with one issue at a time – so I'll stick to one topic. I won't bring a long list to discuss.

Your List

My husband prefers:

1. _____

2. _____

3. _____

4. _____

5. _____

6. _____

7. _____

8. _____

9. _____

Yes, if you are a fast talker – you have probably married the slow talker. If you are person who loves to talk endlessly about every little detail, chances are you have married a quieter type of mate who limits the discussion to the facts.

Unfortunately, knowing what you are like and what your mate is like will not suddenly make you into great communicators. Once you know what your mate is like - his preferences - his style, then you must learn to appreciate and accommodate his differences. A failure to do this will stifle any further growth in this communication aspect of your marriage.

If you resent your husband for his differing communication style and are determined to change *his* behaviour, expect many problems and very limited growth in your marriage.

*C*ommunication Roadblocks

While some people never talk about sex, many couples are less inhibited. However, even these couples, sometimes experience communication roadblocks. Some of them may be:

A. Keeping your spouse guessing

B. Sarcasm and criticism

C. Impersonal terminology

D. Generalizing

A. Keeping Your Spouse Guessing

Many individuals give their partners only vague hints about their sexual needs and don't share enough personal information and detail. Their partners are obliged to fill in the blanks or read their minds. I remember Simon sharing early in our marriage, "There are a lot of things I can do, but one thing I *can't* do is read your mind. If you don't tell me, I don't know - simple as that!"

"I want you to love me better," would be an example of this kind of communication roadblock. That comment could have several interpretations. Partners need to be specific and share examples of how they feel their mate can improve, and specify actions they would like them to take.

The following statements reflect the feelings of some men I've questioned regarding this issue:

"If my wife won't tell me what she wants, then how should I know?"

"My spouse says she likes everything. Surely she must have favorites. This vague response leaves me hanging."

"I really don't think my wife has ever taken the time to think about what *her* needs are. I don't think she knows herself what she wants from me. I know she is not happy, but how do I help?"

"My mate is so shy and embarrassed. I can't get her to even talk about sex, let alone tell me how to improve."

Sometimes men interpret these kind of answers as an "I don't really care" message and this serves as a great frustration for them. Both partners need to be specific in their wishes and preferences.

"WILL YOU **PLEASE** CUT YOUR TOENAILS ?!!"

© *Copyright John McPherson (Used by permission)*

B. Sarcasm And Criticism

Many individuals allow their frustrations about sex to build up until they explode, and then share many unkind, hurtful remarks. Criticism of your partner's lovemaking ability or style, if it is done in a harsh and unloving way, can create a wound that may take months or maybe years to heal.

Derogatory comments about his weight, penis size, or physique can be very damaging.

"*I WISH YOU'D RENEW YOUR MEMBERSHIP AT THE HEALTH CLUB.*"

© *John McPherson (Used by permission)*

One man, as a result of medical problems, was unable to maintain an erection. He was devastated when his wife made a thoughtless, caustic remark disguised as a joke.

We can constructively criticize our partner if it is done in a loving, non-threatening manner. A healthy, Christ-like relationship has *no* room for verbal abuse or sarcasm.

C. Impersonal or Vulgar Terminology

Partners should discuss sexual issues in a personal manner and use appropriate terminology. Some spouses say, "Let's have sex." Many women find this phraseology too impersonal. "Make love or share our love" may be a more desirable way to state their intentions.

One woman reported her husband frequently said, "I want *it*." She often questioned, "Does he want 'it' or ME!?" Depersonalized sexual comments like this carry none of this deeper meaning.

Some partners also use crass or vulgar terminology for genitals or sexual activities. It is a great turn-off for some partners when these terms are used in the bedroom.

You and your spouse may wish to list the clinical terms of male/female anatomy and then discuss how you will be referring to them in a way that is appropriate or pleasing to both partners. Simon and I have developed our own "code" words to describe various body parts. This language of our own adds to the uniqueness and secretiveness of our relationship.

D. *Generalizing*

Generalizing occurs when individuals criticize each other and imply that the problems occur *all* the time. The words 'never', 'always', 'all', and 'any' should be used with great caution.

"You're *never* in a sexy mood."

"You men are *all* alike!"

"You *always* fall asleep right after we make love."

"You *never* think about my needs."

"You're *always* pressuring me to have sex."

The use of the word "I" as opposed to "you" is also desirable. Stating your desires in a *positive* statement of need is better than the negative approach.

For example:

Generalization: "You *never* want sex."

Positive Statement of Need/Desire: "I'd really like to make love to you tonight."

Generalization: "You *never* take the time for me to become aroused; it's always straight to intercourse."

Positive Statement of Need/Desire: "I really like it when you caress and fondle me for a long time before intercourse... You really know how to turn me on and light my fire."

Generalization: "You *never* talk to me – *all* you want is sex."

<u>Positive Statement of Need/Desire</u>: "I really appreciated you taking some time to share some feelings before we made love last night. I feel we connected in spirit, not just our bodies alone."

If your husband was approached in a more loving, respectful manner, the potential for positive change would be greater and he would not be offended or hurt by your generalizations or criticisms.

Helpful Approaches

A. Use Of Questionnaires

Simon and I had done some reading and chatting about sexual intimacy before we were married. However, with our added parental and work responsibilities, we didn't have conversations about our sex life *regularly* after marriage.

After resolving to concentrate on our sexual relationship, I decided to ask Simon a number of thought-provoking questions.

By preparing questions in advance, our conversations became focused and this enabled us to address issues methodically.

These conversations took place while on a leisurely walk, in the car, or during late-night "pillow talk."

If you choose to use questionnaires, do not insist that your husband be seated for lengthy periods of time while you interrogate him. Approach these sharing times in a way that is most comfortable for you both. (See pages 218-225 for possible questions to ask.)

B. Open-Ended Sentences

Not everyone will respond to direct questions well, so another approach may include giving your partner a number of incomplete sentences and then asking him to respond. Some examples might include:

- One of the best sexual memories I have is...
- One of my favorite sexual fantasies with you, my wife, is...
- A sexual activity I would like us to experiment with is...
- You really turn me on when...
- Something that concerns me about our sexual relationship is...
- When I am touched I feel...
- The most exciting, romantic evening for me would consist of...[3]

Remember ...

Change your thoughts, Change your life!

Questions To Ask

Before Having An Intimate Discussion

Do You Have The Right Motives?

If you are asking these questions with the wholesome intention of inquiring how *you* can improve, then proceed. If you are asking the questions as a forum to vent your dissatisfaction and anger, then save your breath. The discussion will take you nowhere. It will result in a heated and unproductive exchange.

Did You Choose The Right Time For Discussion?

If your husband has had a bad or tiring day at work, then it probably isn't the right time to have a discussion along these lines. Being insensitive to his moods and feelings can make these conversations a chore instead of a pleasure. Just because you are in the mood to talk about it, doesn't mean he is.

© *John McPherson (Used by permission)*

Did You Choose The Right Place?

Have you chosen a private setting where you can talk openly and freely without fear of interruption by listening children or the ever-present cell phone?

Are You Prepared To Really Listen?

Do you plan to listen intently, *without interruption,* to your mate? Try not to comment after each of his responses; otherwise, he will feel judged and analyzed rather than sincerely listened to.

If you are a fast thinker/talker, married to a slower thinker/talker, monitor the conversation to make sure your partner is with you. You may be forging on ahead in the conversation only to find out that you lost him after the first point. Slow down your rate of delivery, stick to one topic, and leave more air space for your partner to jump into the conversation. (Simon says I can talk faster than the speed of light!) Your husband may relate to this man's statement: "My wife and I had words, but I didn't get a chance to use mine!" Give your partner an opportunity to act as a mirror, reflecting back the content and overall tone of the message.

It may feel like an eternity when your spouse is silent before answering your question, but give your partner this space. If you continue to dominate the conversation, he will eventually drop out and tune out.

If you are a slow thinker/talker, give your mate some clues that you are with him in the conversation. Instead of remaining silent for long periods of time, consciously endeavor to make comments that let him know you are still engaged in actively listening.

For example:

"I have heard what you have just said; give me a minute to digest it."

"I can't think of a response to what you just said. I'll get back to you tomorrow."

"Stop right here; I can't continue in this conversation. I'm still processing what you said five minutes ago."

Some slow thinkers take a great deal of time to explore every possible nuance of what you have said and won't be prepared to give on-the-spot answers. (This may be very annoying to the "bottom-line, straight-to-the-point" type of person.) It is important to remember this; otherwise, you may feel that he is disinterested. That may not always be the case. [4]

Are You Prepared For One-Word Answers?

Most men aren't as verbal as women and state their opinions in a brief and succinct fashion. This does not necessarily mean they are disinterested; rather, it is simply the way they communicate.

Can You Appreciate The Fact That Your Husband May Feel Very Uncomfortable Talking About These Matters?

Perhaps your mate was not given permission by his parents to verbalize feelings regarding his sexuality. Respect his need for privacy, but at the same time assure him you wish to understand him to a greater degree. He will appreciate your loving interest in him.

Self-disclosure is extremely threatening and many males are hesitant to expose their true feelings for fear of ridicule and rejection.

Are You Interrogating Or Are You Sensitively Asking Questions?

Remember, the tone of your voice and body language will give a clear message – either positive or negative. Try not to be too aggressive. Don't talk for too fast, too long or put words in his mouth.

Are You Prepared For The Fact That These Conversations May Give Vent To A Wide Range Of Emotions? Are You Listening For Feelings As Well As Words?

These discussions might provoke anger, tears, defensiveness, rebellion, and/or feelings of inadequacy. Are you prepared to risk experiencing these possible reactions? As your partner slowly processes this information, you may have to suffer through "the silent treatment" for a while. Remember, marriages may be made in heaven, but so are thunder and lightning.

Be tenacious, though. Just because one conversation doesn't go well, it doesn't mean that you should no longer pursue such conversations. If you perceive the conversation is going nowhere or heading in the wrong direction, accept that fact. Start again. Apologize, if appropriate. Respond by saying, "I'm sorry I reacted negatively to our discussion yesterday. Can we try again? Let me endeavour to express my feelings in a manner that won't be hurtful or offensive to you."

If you don't give each other permission to be totally honest, your conversations will be shallow and unproductive.

Also be prepared to read between the lines and be sensitive to underlying "feeling" messages. Understanding the hidden messages behind words is often difficult. As you listen for feelings, observe body language, including posture, facial expressions, and gestures. Hopefully, you will communicate more effectively.

Are You Prepared to Respond With a Change in Action And Attitude as a Result of the Conversation?

If you are merely collecting data *without* the desire to really change, then discard your questionnaire. Be aware that your partner may reflect your area(s) of weakness in his comments, and you may not care to hear this. If, as a result of this meaningful conversation, your marriage has improved, then it is well worth the risk of being hurt or even offended by his comments.

Have You Spent Some Concerted Time In Prayer Before Such Conversations, Asking The Lord To Direct Your Words And Comments?

"May the words of my mouth and the meditation of my heart be pleasing in your sight, O Lord." Psalms 19:14 (KJV). This may be a verse to pray before such interaction. Remember, *"a word aptly spoken is like apples of gold in settings of silver."* Proverbs 25:11 (NIV).

Note:

The following questions should *not necessarily* be asked all *at once*. These are sample questions you may wish to explore *over time*. Some of these questions will need to be altered slightly if your husband is not a Christian, or they may not be applicable to you at all. Be selective in the questions you ask.

Exploring His Family History

1. Could you share a few adjectives that would describe the family you were raised in? (e.g., close-knit, angry, abusive, loving...)

2. Could you tell me about your relationship with your mother? Describe it to me. What did you like or dislike about her?

3. Could you tell me about your relationship with your father? Describe it to me. What did you like or dislike about him?

4. How would you describe your parents' marriage relationship? Excellent? Very good? Fair? Poor?

5. How do you think your parents related sexually? In your opinion, do you think they had a fulfilling relationship?

6. Did your parents express affection in front of you? In what manner? How did that make you feel?

7. What were the names you used for your genitals as a child?

8. Did your parents talk about sexual issues with you? When and how?

9. Did they feel comfortable talking about the subject?

10. Did they give you permission to ask questions of them regarding this subject or were you stifled in this area of sexuality?

11. Did your parents make you feel guilty or ashamed when you mentioned sexual matters?

12. Did your parents scold you when they caught you talking about sex? Fondling yourself? Masturbating?

13. Did you masturbate? How did you feel about that?

14. How did you learn about how children are conceived? Did your parents tell you? If not, who did?

15. How was nudity handled in your home?

16. What was your earliest sexual memory?

17. Were you ever exposed to pornography as a child/youth?

18. Were there other individuals in your life who exposed you to dirty jokes, or vulgar sexual talk and language?

19. As a child or youth, were you ever exposed to a sexual activity with another adolescent or adult that made you feel uncomfortable?

20. Can you recall any traumatic sexual experience(s) in your life? Sexual abuse of any kind?

21. Were your parents Christians?

22. Did your parents give you the impression that God approved of sex or did they make you feel that it was a carnal, dirty activity?

23. Did your parents provide you with any helpful, educational literature about sex?

Questions About The Sex Experience Itself

1. When is your favorite time to make love? Morning? Evening? (Don't be surprised if he tells you *any time* is the right time!)

2. What kind of relaxation gets you "in the mood?"

3. Do you prefer to talk before making love?

4. Do you prefer to talk during sex?

5. Do you like to talk immediately after sex or debrief the next morning?

6. Do you enjoy explicit sex talk? Is there anything that offends you?

7. Do you like to eat and drink before, during, or after making love?

8. Where do you like to be touched?

9. How do you like to be touched there? Can you share some suggestions?

10. Do you feel comfortable with the way I touch you or is my approach irritating at times?

11. Which areas do you not enjoy being touched?

12. Do you prefer me to initiate? Or do you find that intimidating?

13. Do you fancy being undressed by me? Or prefer to do it yourself?

14. Do you enjoy a massage? What makes this experience most pleasurable for you?

15. Do you prefer to make love with the lights on? Off?

16. What kind of special lighting do you find conducive to an appealing atmosphere?

17. Do you enjoy making love with your eyes closed or do you prefer eye contact?

18. Do you prefer the curtains open or shut? Window open or shut? Door open or shut?

19. Do you wish to explore new lovemaking positions? If yes, which ones?

20. How would you suggest we improve our sexual technique?

21. What is the best aspect of our present sex life?

22. What can I do to make our love expression(s) more pleasurable for you?

23. What kinds of activities bring arousal to you the fastest? Which are most pleasurable?

24. Are there any creative props you would like me to use in the bedroom?

25. Would you describe our lovemaking as the same old predictable routine, or spontaneous and passionate?

26. Are you satisfied with the birth control methods we have chosen to use?

27. Do you have any physiological concerns? Do they require medical attention?

28. How many times a week do you think we should make love in order to satisfy your sexual needs? (Keeping in mind, of course, that we both have jobs, children, etc.)

29. (If appropriate) Why don't you want to make love?

Questions About Other Personal Preferences

1. How do you prefer me to dress for bed?

2. What colours of nightwear do you prefer me to wear to bed?

3. What types of fabric do you find most appealing? Flannelette or satin?

4. Would you feel offended if I purchased my own bedroom attire instead of you purchasing it?

5. What kind of undergarments do you prefer me to wear?

6. How do you prefer me to dress in public?

7. How could I improve in this area?

8. What scents turn you on? Identify your favorites.

9. Do you like scented candles?

10. Do you prefer that we shower together before lovemaking?

11. What type of music sets the best mood for lovemaking? Who are your favorite artists? Your favorite selections?

12. Where do you enjoy making love?

13. Is our bedroom an attractive, appealing place to you? Could you share some suggestions for redecorating that would improve our bedroom?

14. Do you like satin sheets? Flannelette sheets? Cotton sheets?

15. Do you feel relaxed in our home? Should we consider putting a lock on our bedroom door to ensure privacy?

16. Where do you fantasize about us making love? (Be prepared for some out-of-this-world answers to this one, girls!)

Other Questions

1. Do you think I am willing to improve? Do you think I am prepared to leave my comfort zone to please you?

2. Do you feel we spend enough time talking about our sex life?

3. Do you sense that I really understand your sexual needs and your physiological makeup? If not, will you help me understand?

4. Do you feel I respect your sexual limitations? (Perhaps due to illness, aging, physiological problems, or other significant traumatic events.) Are you experiencing an abnormal degree of stress that I should be sensitive to at this time?

5. How do you feel about your own body appearance and build?

6. How do you think I feel about your physical appearance?

7. Have I ever made fun of you? Have any of my words regarding your sexual prowess hurt or offended you?

8. Do you feel confident that you are meeting my sexual needs?

9. Do you feel I have ever violated your trust and shared information about our sex life with others? If yes, please explain.

10. Are there issues that are adversely affecting our sex life that we need to resolve outside the bedroom?

11. Do you feel we are saving our best energy for each other? Do you feel we are putting enough time and effort into our sexual life?

12. Should we consider reading an informative book on sexual relations or attending a helpful seminar that would enrich our ongoing sex life?

13. Do you feel affirmed by my lovemaking to you? Do I praise you enough?

14. Do you feel our sex life is improving gradually and has been a growth area in our marriage?

15. Do you feel comfortable sharing your deepest, most intimate feelings with me or is that an uncomfortable or threatening experience?

16. Do you feel I compare you with others? Perhaps past spouses?

17. Do you think we should consider seeking professional Christian counselling to help us in an area of need in our sexual relationship? Would you be open to that?

18. What are your top five needs? Where does sexual fulfillment rank on your list?

Asking these kinds of questions, with the right motive and at the right time and place, can help improve your sex life immensely. Let me share selectively from some of the conversations Simon and I have had.

On one occasion Simon asked, "Why don't you wear that expensive perfume I buy you?" My response was, "Well, dear, I really appreciate and value the Eternity™ and Opium™ you purchase for me, but I only wear it on special occasions. I can't flaunt it around the house!" Simon replied, "Why not? I bought it for you. I love the smell of that fragrance on you. If your supply runs out, I'll buy you more."

My reply was, "That is a valid suggestion, Simon. If you've got the money, honey, I've got the time!"

I was very happy I had taken the time to ask that question, as it helped me understand one of Simon's preferences. With very little effort on my part, I could be assured that I was making him happier. I now squirt his perfume on first thing in the morning, before he comes home from work, and just before heading to bed.

On another occasion, we were discussing the kind of touching we preferred and enjoyed. Simon frequently massaged my feet and he thought he was doing a loving action to help relax me. The fact of the matter was ...

I hate anyone touching my feet! If someone gave me a free pedicure, I would turn it down, simply because I don't enjoy it. I had never chosen to talk to him about this because I didn't want to hurt his feelings. When I lovingly shared my preferences, he was very appreciative and said he would be happy to oblige by concentrating on other areas to touch. This open, frank, yet sensitive sharing of feelings helped improve our special times together.

Another evening, I asked him, "What could I do to improve our sex life?" He answered, "Would it be possible for *you to initiate* sexual activities? Don't make *me* always be the pursuer."

I found this comment rather interesting. Undoubtedly I am dating myself when I share the following information, but when I was growing up, women did not initiate romantic activities. My mother did not allow me to phone boys. I certainly never asked males out on dates. I was programmed, like other girls of my generation, that nice girls do *not* pursue men. (My, how things have changed!)

I gave his comments a great deal of thought. As a result, I began reading books and magazine articles, and using my own imagination to develop some new, creative ways to initiate sexual activities. I also began meditating on the Shulamite woman described in Scripture. I found she was responsive, adventurous, uninhibited, and expressive.[5] She served as a good role model for me! (A full description of some of my ideas can be found in my other book, *Romance 101: 101 Creative and Fun Ideas to Keep Your Marriage Alive and Sparking!* (See back of book for details in Appendix.)

Because of my willingness to honestly and openly dialogue with Simon regarding these matters, our marriage has been greatly enhanced and enriched.

Because we have chosen to have these conversations in a relaxed, non-threatening manner, we have often had a good chuckle while chatting. I remember on one occasion, I asked him to cue me on how I could touch him in a more pleasurable fashion. After hearing his reply, I said, "Oh I get it. You want me to play Simon Says."

"Simon says do this!"

"Simon says do that!"

Now **What?**

After you have had a meaningful conversation regarding your sex life:

- Review your answers and prioritize what areas you want to address first. If you are a newlywed, rest assured that you are not going to perfect your lovemaking during the first year. Just like any other area of your marriage, learning and changing is a lifelong process. Remember, practice makes perfect and most men are delighted to show up for practice!

- Schedule when you can discuss in detail *one* aspect of your conversation. There may be many other related deeper issues that should be addressed. Don't just uncover them and fail to pursue corrective action. Plan to spend quality time talking about those issues, arrange for counselling if necessary, or purchase some informative books that will assist in working through your area(s) of need.

- Undoubtedly, you will have identified areas in which you have opposite preferences. If one partner clearly enjoys making love at night and the other spouse fancies first thing in the morning, you are going to have to negotiate and find alternate times that suit both of you – maybe at noon, Saturday or Sunday afternoon.

WALT NORDMAN WAS NOT A MORNING PERSON.

© Copyright John McPherson (Used by permission)

When Simon and I encounter absolute deadlocks in some of these areas, we have resorted to taking turns. We share, "Tonight it is *your night* to do things *your way* and I will be a willing, active, enthusiastic participant, and the next time it will be done *my way*." The most important consideration is that you *respect* your spouse's feelings. We decided early in our marriage that we would never ask our mate to do anything that made either of us feel uncomfortable – *no* questions asked. That is not to say that we have not both left our comfort zones at times, but we always go with the wishes of the more conservative partner – and don't lay any guilt trips.

We have come to the realization that we will not always get exactly what we desire – and we can appreciate that fact. We feel as long as we are not stagnating and that we are putting considerable effort into meeting the other's needs, then we are satisfied. While we have a great desire to improve in this area, it has not become an obsession or been pursued to the point that we can't have fun and enjoy our times together without pressure.

Conclusion

Your ability to talk openly and with total honesty about your sexual life is key to a passionate, growing sex life! It will take time – it is a life-long project, but well worth the effort.

Life-Changing Questions to Ponder

♥ Do you and your mate find it difficult to talk about your sex life? If yes, why?

♥ Have you taken the time to explore with your husband the questions shared in this chapter?

♥ Can you identify each other's communication style and preferences?

♥ Which of the communication roadblocks mentioned in this chapter have you experienced?

♥ Do you need to schedule an intimate conversation (at the right time and place and with the right motives)?

The Life-Changing Word...
Memorize/Meditate

"A wise (wo)man's words express deep streams of thought." Proverbs 18:4 (TLB - adapted).

♦ ♦ ♦

"A gentle answer turns away wrath,
but a harsh word stirs up anger."
Proverbs 15:1 (NIV).

♦ ♦ ♦

"Some people like to make cutting remarks,
but the words of the wise soothe and heal."
Proverbs 12:18 (TLB).

"A friendly discussion is as stimulating as the sparks
that fly when iron strikes iron."
Proverbs 27:17 (TLB).

♦ ♦ ♦

"In the end, people appreciate frankness more than
flattery." Proverbs 28:23 (TLB).

♦ ♦ ♦

"The wise (wo)man learns by listening."
Proverbs 12:11 (TLB adapted).

♦ ♦ ♦

"Don't refuse to accept criticism, get all the help
you can get." Proverbs 23:12 (TLB).

♦ ♦ ♦

"A good (wo)man thinks before she speaks."
Proverbs 15:28 (TLB - adapted).

♦ ♦ ♦

"Kind words are like honey – enjoyable and beautiful."
Proverbs 16:24 (TLB).

My Prayer to the
Life-Changer

Dear God: After reading this chapter, I...

_____

_____

_____

_____

Chapter Seven

How to Plan Your Sex Life

MEETING...

*"Scheduling increases
anticipation and
anticipation sparks passion."*
Clifford & Joyce Penner [1]

Let The Women Speak:

♥ "Plan your sex life? You've got to be kidding."

♥ "Who has the time to plan anything? I'm so busy; I'm too exhausted!"

♥ "I think if I plan my sex life it will become mechanical and boring."

♥ "Why does everything have to be my responsibility?"

♥ "I thought lovemaking and sexual encounters were supposed to be spontaneous and natural."

These statements may be true, but if your lifestyle is anything like mine, you will have to make your sex life a priority, *plan* it, and schedule time on your calendar.

Let me explain how I started working on this area (Stay with me... it was quite a journey.)

☞isappointed Again

It was a typical January. I sat down and reflected on my life during the past year and pondered what I hoped to accomplish in the new one. Regrettably, I was again disappointed that over the course of the year I had not followed through with my very noble and worthwhile goals written the previous January. I was increasingly disgusted and disappointed with myself for losing my focus throughout the year.

Admittedly, I had accomplished a number of things, but I was disturbed that a great deal of my energy had been spent meeting the needs of others - serving to enhance their goals and agenda (which were often very worthwhile), but often at the expense of achieving my own goals and personal priorities.

$\mathscr{L}$ife Is Not A Rehearsal!

Shortly after this time of reflection, I listened to John Maxwell's tape, entitled "Life: It's Worth Doing." [2]
He stated,

"You only live once.
But if you do it right, once is enough."
(Author Unknown)

Other quotes I reflected on were:

"Life is not a rehearsal –
you have to do it right the first time!"
(Author Unknown)

235

"Life is like a penny – you can spend it any way you want, but you can only spend it once."

I then listened to a tape by Tim Elmore, *"Living the Life You Were Meant to Live,"* which relates the story of Alfred Nobel. [3]

One day Alfred Nobel opened his newspaper to see that *his* obituary was in the newspaper (they had printed *his* instead of his brother's). The obituary read, "Alfred Nobel, the inventor of dynamite, enabled the world to kill more people in wartime than in any time in the past. He died a very rich man."

Alfred was stunned and horrified that this is what he was going to be remembered for. He quickly decided that because he was still alive, he must change that legacy. As we know, he became the creator of the Nobel Peace Prize that recognizes the outstanding effort of individuals working to achieve world peace.

He later stated, "Everyone deserves an opportunity to change their obituary midcourse."

*W*rite Your Own Obituary

Tim Elmore asked, "What do you really want to be remembered for? Would people remember you for the important things you accomplished? What would your family and those closest to you relate?"

These questions really challenged me. While I was living a consistent Christian life and had healthy, strong relationships with my husband, children, and other family members, I felt I had to take some time to contemplate what I would like shared at my funeral.

Tim instructed me to write my own obituary. He said, "Visualize that you are sitting in the back row of your church, listening to the eulogy and tributes shared about you. Would you agree with what they were saying? Were they having to 'stretch the truth' somewhat to make you appear like an outstanding individual? Were they highlighting accomplishments that *you* considered important? Did your life really make a difference and add value to others?"

**"Everyone deserves an opportunity
to change their obituary midcourse."**

Alfred Nobel

The
Obituary Of

_____

_____

_____

_____

_____

_____

_____

_____

_____

_____

_____

THE GREATEST USE OF LIFE IS TO SPEND IT
ON SOMETHING THAT WILL OUTLAST IT!

- William James

By spending some time in reflection, I reviewed my life thoroughly. What was I doing with my time, energy, and money and was it *exactly* what God intended? It was a very challenging and thought-provoking exercise, and it resulted in the completion of a significant list of things I wished to be remembered for.

What Were My Top Three Objectives?

Next, I asked myself this question: What are my top three objectives and how am I actively seeking to meet them? My top three were:

♥ I wanted God to say I had accomplished His intended purpose in my life, utilizing it for His glory. I wanted to realize my full potential and make a significant difference in His kingdom. (My life's motto has been a quote by William James: "The greatest use of life is to spend it on something that will outlast it.")

♥ I wanted Simon to share that I was an outstanding wife.

♥ I hoped my children would say I was a committed and wonderful mother.

I have always agreed with this statement by John Maxwell about success:

"Success is when the people who know you the best, love and respect you the most." 4

239

My family members are the individuals who know the real me. I can sometimes fool those on the outside, but I can't misrepresent myself to my closest relatives. Their evaluation is of utmost importance!

Although I had a long list of other priorities for myself and my career, if I scored poorly in one of these top three, my other accomplishments meant next to nothing.

One of my top three objectives was that I wanted to be remembered as a devoted and loving wife – a wife who kept Simon supremely happy and fulfilled as a result of my attention.

This goal may not seem startling or unusual, yet I had to honestly ask myself "Do I really put my money where my mouth is?" Do I really put the time and energy into our relationship that it deserves, or do I just give it lip service and my leftover attention?"

My desire was that my husband would affirm the following about me:

- ❤ That I had been his best friend, supporter, cheerleader, and confidante.
- ❤ That he was proud of me for my character and my accomplishments.
- ❤ That I had had been a good keeper of our home.
- ❤ That I had been great lover and met his sexual needs to the fullest.

♥ That he was delighted to come home – to his castle, his haven, his oasis.

♥ That I was fellow dreamer, a kindred spirit, and that I had been an outstanding supporting cast, helping him achieve his life's goals.

♥ That we enjoyed a great deal of fun and frivolity together.

♥ That I was a wonderful mother to our children.

But... was I really prioritizing enough time in my schedule to accomplish these very desirable goals to the degree of success that I intended?

*P*urchase A Five-Segment Scribbler

Here's a game plan that I developed that may work for you. Purchase a scribbler and divide it into five sections. Entitle the sections:

♥ My plans – Me and God

♥ My plans – Me and my own personal goals

♥ My plans – Me and my husband

♥ My plans – Me and my children (if applicable)

♥ My plans – Me and my vocation

In each section, begin creating a calendar for the next 12 weeks, and list attainable, measurable, observable, realistic statements of intent. For example: I will, in the next twelve weeks...

Each section should focus on two or three items to address, rather than containing a vast list of goals you are trying to accomplish. (If you attempt to simultaneously achieve many objectives, you may be overwhelmed and accomplish little.)

By making a list and formulating a game plan for improvement, you will keep focused and your grand and wonderful intentions *will* materialize.

Consistently taking the time to do this will result in greater success and progress in achieving your important goals. If your goals are too lofty, you will soon realize this and then be able to rewrite them for the next 12 weeks.

So **What Does This Have To Do With Your Sex Life?**

You may have a growing and healthy marriage, but perhaps feel you need to give more concerted attention and effort to many areas of your relationship. If your husband is to be a *top* priority, then you must *schedule* some time and energy for him.

Jobs, committees, and friends may come and go. Don't overlook or neglect what is really important. Investing your time and energy in your husband will result in *outstanding* returns.

If this reflects your concerns, you may need to readjust or rethink your priorities and ensure your husband is on the top of your list, after God and before your children.

$\mathcal{S}$o What Are His Needs?

Willard Harley suggests in his book, *His Needs, Her Needs,* that the top five needs of a man are:

1. Sexual fulfillment
2. Recreational companionship
3. An attractive spouse
4. Domestic support (housekeeping, childcare)
5. Admiration [5]

These may or may not be the top five needs of your husband, so take the time to ask what his needs are. You may be surprised at his answers. Whatever his responses may be, it will give you some direction as to what he is desiring you to contribute to your marital relationship.

$\mathcal{H}$ave A Planning Meeting

With Your Husband

Identify your husband's needs. Refer to his responses to the questions you shared with him in Chapter 6. Then purpose to:

1. Systematically evaluate his answers. Ask him to identify which ones were most important to him. These will become your top priority and receive immediate attention.

2. Create a "to-do" list. Recording these goals on paper is of utmost importance. If you merely verbalize your intentions, you will forget what you discussed, lose sight of your priorities, and have no guide with which to monitor your progress and success.

Where Am I Going To Get The Time?

The biggest roadblock you will have in reaching some of these goals is the age-old problem of little time, little energy!

While this is not a book on time management, let me share some of the things you could do to utilize your time more effectively.

♥ Monitor your time much more closely. I'm sure it must have been a mother who said, "The harder I work, the behinder I get." People in the time management field suggest that 80 percent of the things we do each day yield 20 percent of the results. With this in mind, identify where your time is being spent. Begin to keep track of your daily time usage for a two-week period. Start to look for time-wasters and try to consolidate jobs.

"Work Smarter – Not Harder."

A few suggestions to consider are:

♥ Phone your friends and relatives on their birthdays and anniversaries instead of sending cards. Another great time-saving option is to send cards over the Internet, especially to those overseas or out of the country.

♥ Purchase multiple gifts for children's birthday parties or baby showers in advance.

♥ Buy toiletries and groceries in bulk.

♥ Purchase Christmas gifts by shopping on-line or at seasonal sales.

♥ Handle each piece of mail only once. If it is not important, it should go directly into the garbage. If it must be kept, file it right away.

♥ Put all your household bills on automatic payment withdrawals each month. This will save a great deal of time and concern regarding due dates.

♥ Listen to teaching and enrichment tapes on your Walkman™ while powerwalking, jogging, or driving the car.

♥ Stop watching TV, or at least not as much. This can be a huge time-waster, adding little value to your life.

Record how much time you watch TV in a week – it may surprise you.

❤ Be more selective of the opportunities you pursue or commit yourself to. In my younger years, I felt that any open door of opportunity was orchestrated by God. I have changed my thoughts in this regard. When asked to serve on committees, I tactfully say "no" more often. This has been a real challenge for me because I love to be involved, but I found that I was often over-extended at my own personal sacrifice and the expense of quality time with Simon and our children.

❤ Make a "to-do" list every day. It will help you focus on your day's events and what you would like to accomplish.

❤ Let your answering machine take your calls. If you have an important project you want to give your best time and attention to, let the phone ring and respond to all your calls later.

❤ Be a better delegator. Enlist the help of others to accomplish your projects.

Romantic Reflections

Keeping a *personal* calendar, noting my romantic plans and sexual encounters, has assisted me in keeping more focused and accountable to my goals.

On my Romantic Reflections Calendar (See Figure 2), I record:

- ♥ Our special love moments together this month.
- ♥ A special sexual event I initiated.
- ♥ How I admired/affirmed my husband this month (gift, card, words, etc.)
- ♥ My emotional response when he came home.

These simple, yet meaningful, notations take only seconds to write. This is not a detailed project.

If, at the end of the month, I don't observe many notations, I know that I have simply been too busy and that I haven't saved enough time and energy for Simon. (Conversely, Simon may also have been too busy and not scheduled enough time for us.) Of course, life has its upsets – sickness, deaths, busy times of year - which rearrange the best laid plans, but I have discovered that making these simple notations has prevented me from neglecting this area for long periods of time.

I concur with what sex therapist Dr. Janet Wolfe shares, "Anything worth doing is worth scheduling – especially things that require some time and space and freedom from distraction. We schedule activities all the time, from tennis games and plays to grease jobs on our cars. Surely sex is just as important to our physical and mental well-being, not to mention our relationship, as these other activities." [6]

I also record the one or two things Simon and I are working on that month to improve our sexual life, or perhaps the name of a book, article, or tape we have listened to that month.

(P.S. We also work on other areas of our marriage, such as: parenting skills, communication skills, etc. It may seem, from reading this book, that we have a singular focus and spend all our time in the bedroom. *Not so.)*

ℛemember ...

Change your thoughts – Change your life!

♥ *My Romantic Reflections* ♥

Sun	Mon	Tue	Wed	Thu	Fri	Sat
1	2	3	4 ♥	5	6	7
8 ♥	9	10 ☺	11	12 ☺	13	14
15	16	17	18	19	20	21
22	23 ☺	24	25	26 ♥	27	28
29	30	31 ☺				

Figure 2

I will record:
- ♥ Our special love moments together this month. (Use little heart notations ♥♥♥)
- ♥ A special sexual event I initiated.
- ♥ How I admired/affirmed my husband this month (gift, card, words, etc.)
- ♥ My emotional response when he came home. (☺ ☺ ☺)
- ♥ What book or article I/we read
- ♥ How I worked on meeting one of my husband's sexual requests for change.

Plan **Your Daily Encounters**

At least once a day, endeavor to connect with your mate to discuss your day. Talk about the present or the immediate future. This time frame could vary from day to day. Some couples spend these quality moments over a cup of coffee at breakfast, meet for lunch, or connect at bedtime. Many men, who travel extensively with their jobs, phone their wives frequently at a predetermined time to update each other. Each couple will have to carve out time as it is convenient to their own schedules. Sometimes these encounters involve sensuous moments, others not.

Plan **Your Periodic Events**

(Some Call Them Date Nights)

Note the key word here – PLAN! Again, Simon and I get out our monthly calendars and decide when we are going to spend time together on a weekly basis.

Some books suggest a date night. For us, at this stage in our lives, this plan doesn't work. We have piano lessons, soccer practice, Bible study, Friday family night, homework preparation and as a result, we have difficulty allocating an *evening* for us.

Because Simon's day off is Friday, we have chosen to earmark Friday morning as our time alone. I get up, send our children off to school, and then we turn off the phone, draw the drapes, and do our own thing.

Sometimes we read together in bed, make love, go out for breakfast, go for a walk, go shopping, watch a video together - it varies from week to week. We try not to get in a rut. Sometimes we are simply exhausted and we fall asleep in each other's arms – only to awaken refreshed to do something else.

Seize the moment –
Take time to hone your romantic spirit.

Obviously, this arrangement reflects what works best for us, but you will want to consider sitting down with your husband and asking him what will work best for you both. Perhaps Sunday afternoons or Saturday mornings would be an alternative.

If your husband is away a great deal due to work commitments, you are going to have to utilize the time when he is home to your best advantage. Your number one priority is to reconnect. Ensure other events don't crowd out your special time together. You have to reassess and remind yourselves "Who and what is most important, and what activities you must save some energy for?"

In spite of their hectic schedules, Sue and Bob always looked forward to their weekly date night.

© Copyright Doug Hall (Used by permission)

**"Marriages may be made in heaven,
but the maintenance work is done on earth."**

Author Unknown

Do we have this weekly time without fail? No. Life is not perfect. We regularly make revisions in our plans. If we must postpone our time together for some reason, then we immediately reschedule or play catch-up the next week.

We have changed this time frame periodically to accommodate our ever-changing lifestyle. You may have to do the same.

Plan Your Seasonal Escapes

Monthly getaways have been suggested by some. Unfortunately, time and money constraints to make this impossible for us, so we have chosen a more realistic goal of planning an escape once every twelve weeks, or once a quarter. You will have to choose your own time frame.

Tips For Having A Successful Getaway

1. Plan the Dates Well in Advance

Sit down with your mate and your calendar and decide when your getaway will occur. Remember, a getaway does not necessarily involve an overnight stay. Sometimes the logistics of securing a babysitter or other time constraints make long getaways impossible. Consider half-day or full-day events. Some motels have great reductions on "day only" use of their rooms.

Regardless of what time frame you choose for your event, ensure you both put it on your calendars well in advance and do not reschedule anything on that date, except for mutually agreed upon reasons.

2. Plan Ahead Together

Half the fun of an event is the anticipation of it! Simon and I take turns being in charge of planning our getaway events. This has also been our tradition for our anniversary celebrations. We try to keep the details of the event a surprise in order to increase anticipation!

A getaway is a focused time that gives you a chance to regroup, reignite romance and deepen your marital bond.

3. Decide Where You Will Have Your Getaway

You could consider options such as the following:

♥ Borrow a friend's trailer, tent, motorhome, or cabin for an overnight stay or weekend.

♥ Accompany your husband on a business trip or conference. Two persons can sleep in the same bed for the same price. Consider arranging for a jacuzzi in your room by paying an extra charge. Another option is to go a few days earlier or stay later than the conference in order to have some quality time together.

♥ Borrow the home of friends who are away on holidays. You could return the favor at a later date.

♥ Book a bed and breakfast type of accommodation. Check out the Internet to acquire possible options. This kind of accommodation can usually be found at very reasonable prices.

© Copyright John McPherson (Used by permission)

If you wish to go out of town, then check the Internet, go to a travel agent, or visit the Chamber of Commerce and find out information you need in advance. Go over the brochures and dream together.

If your plans include a stay at a hotel, make sure you communicate your preferences, such as a non-smoking room, one with a jacuzzi, a fireplace, a king-size bed, a view, breakfast in bed, etc. Failure to do this can result in disappointment when you arrive and such amenities are not available. Ask the hotel staff to fax you a copy of your reservation. This may be helpful to you at the check-in counter. Also, if for some reason they can't supply all the amenities you have pre-booked, the hotel may offer you a free meal or upgrade your room due to of the mix-up.

Fail to plan

or...

plan to fail.

"FOR PETE'S SAKE, STELLA, WATERBEDS ARE PERFECTLY SAFE!"

© Copyright John McPherson (Used by permission)

Ensure you have a map. Having clear directions to your destination can help you avoid many heated discussions.

"TAKE THE NEXT RIGHT."

Do everything possible to make your trip enjoyable.

"WHOOPS! SORRY I MISSED THAT REST AREA. OH, WELL. THE SIGN SAYS THERE'S ANOTHER ONE IN 76 MILES."

4. Discuss In Advance What The Goals, Expectations, And Purpose(s) Of This Getaway Will Be

The reason for your getaway could include:

♥ A total rest and relaxation, "do nothing" event - plenty of sleep, peace, and quietness.

♥ A special prayer time together to pray through our upcoming year or an important decision.

♥ A "sex and seclusion" event. - Take along a new "how to be a better lover" type of book and hone your lovemaking skills.

♥ A time of discussion. Reflect on your finances, children, jobs, and goal-setting for the future.

♥ A time to work through a weak area of your marriage. (I know one couple who plan this type of event once a year. They do this *before* they go on their summer vacation, so that any pressing or pertinent issues are dealt with before vacation time. This way "the air has been cleared" for a great, stress-free holiday time.)

♥ A recreational event (swimming, hiking, golfing, biking, etc.)

♥ An entertainment opportunity - Enjoy a concert, fair, sporting event, or exhibition.

♥ A sight-seeing adventure to explore some new territory.

A getaway can include a *combination* of several of these things. They don't have to be intense, structured events, but there are times when you will want to set some predetermined goals.

Sorting this out *before* you leave home will avoid dissatisfaction later. If one partner envisions that all you are going to do is sit by the pool and drink soda, while the other anticipates a non-stop shopping or sightseeing trip, expect conflict and disappointment.

The primary consideration is, don't overplan. If every second is planned and accounted for, it won't seem like much of a break from your normal routine. Have structure - not bondage.

Keep your events simple - simple is less stressful and much more relaxing.

This acrostic might help:

S – selective

I – intimate

M – meaningful

P – pleasant

L – loving

E – exhilarating and exciting!

5. Use A Theme When Planning Special Events

For example: For one of our anniversary getaways, I chose a "*Royal* Rendezvous" theme. I rented a room in the *Royal* Edmonton Hotel, bought matching bathrobes for my "King" and I, had chocolates, fruit, and drinks delivered to the room on a silver platter, and gave Simon the *royal* treatment all weekend.

6. Plan for Some Private, Personal Time

On some occasions, we have scheduled some free time for each of us to do what we wished to, on our own. Simon and I aren't "joined at the hip" and we can both "do our own thing" for a while and find that refreshing. For example, Simon may golf for a few hours while I read a book by the pool. We later meet back together for a meal and other entertainment.

Some men may resist going on getaways, because they think it will be too intense, too much time together, too much talking, and too much pressure to keep busy every second. They may also feel that you are going to "get on their case" about some issue(s) and there will be no way for them to escape. If this reflects your husband's feelings, then adapt and adjust your schedule and expectations accordingly.

7. Establish Ground Rules

Depending on the goals of your getaway, predetermine issues like:

❤ No discussion about your children, in-laws, friends, or home concerns. Avoid all controversial and potentially disruptive topics.

❤ No discussion about jobs/vocations

Other considerations might include:

❤ No briefcases.

❤ No calls to your job, no cell phones, and only one phone call home per day

❤ No TV. - No sports.

❤ No shopping.

❤ No attention to adhering to diets.

❤ No pre-determined schedule. Sleep and eat when you feel like it. (If you live in a time-driven lifestyle, as we do, these kinds of weekends are lifesavers.)

8. Budget Ahead for Such Events

We have a fund that we call "Fun Money." We set aside some money on a monthly basis. Sometimes our getaways are very inexpensive, while other times we choose to save up for them. You must discuss what the budget for the getaway will be. That will ensure that each partner knows the limits in advance.

One couple put a dollar in a special jar each time they made love. They were saving to go on a special trip for their 25th wedding anniversary. (This would be a great incentive to make love more often, girls!)

9. Make Sure All The Necessary Details Are Cared For At Home Well In Advance

When babysitting is necessary, contact Grandma or a friend well in advance. If you require someone to care for your pet, pick up the mail, or drive your child to various sporting and club events, attend to these details in plenty of time. Caring for these details at the last minute can create a great deal of extra stress.

10. Be Well Rested Before You Go On Your Getaway

Plan to get to bed early the night before such an event. This will ensure you are both refreshed beforehand. This may not always happen, of course. I can recall one occasion when Simon and I were both exhausted when we arrived at our destination. We crawled into bed for an afternoon nap, slept off some stresses, and then were ready to party for the night.

11. Use Coupons And Discount Books

Entertainment™ Books or other discount books allow for great price reductions and make these events more affordable.

12. Create Some Suspense And Give Your Partner A Sense Of Your Great Anticipation

On one occasion when it was my turn to plan the event, I left Sweet Escape™ chocolate bars on Simon's car seat, on his desk, in his shoes with little notes stating I was looking forward to our getaway. I have also asked him to participate in a treasure hunt around the house, searching for clues regarding our destination.

Have great "sex-pectations."

13. Don't Let Your Children Discourage You

Children can be very possessive and manipulative at times. While they are extremely important people in your life, so is your marital relationship. Both relationships deserve some quality time.

Occasionally, our children have protested, stating that they wanted to join us, but we tell them, "Let us go alone; we'll come back better parents, more relaxed and healthier." We often allow our children special privileges while we are gone. (Staying up extra-late or allowing them to go to a special event often serves as a trade-off for them not coming along.)

14. Prepare the Setting

Ensure that your getaway will be a romantic rendezvous. Create an atmosphere conducive to intimacy. Be sure to take along romantic mood music, candles, lotions, satin sheets, favourite food and drinks, alluring bedroom attire, etc.

15. Pray About All The Details Of Your Event

The Lord can bless all your plans and make it so much more memorable. Plan to spend some time praying together with your mate on your getaway. Remember - spiritual intimacy and physical intimacy go hand-in-hand.

The closer you are to God...

the closer you will become to your mate.

16. Prepare Your Mind

As your getaway approaches, start relaxing and begin unwinding. Prepare your thoughts and start to change gears. If one purpose of your getaway is to enjoy uninterrupted sexual delights, then start to think sexual thoughts. Let your sanctified imagination go and daydream about the upcoming fulfillment of your fantasies with your lover. Prepare for passion...

"IT HELPS ME TO UNWIND."

© Copyright John McPherson (Used by permission)

Marriage is like an empty box.

It remains empty unless you put more in

than you take out.

(Author Unknown)

17. After Your Arrival Home From Your Special Event

Take time to give your mate a note that tells him what your favorite aspects of the getaway were, and share that you were really delighted to have his undivided attention for those few hours or days. This appreciation will go a long way in setting the stage for another similar event.

18. What To Do If You Are Married To A Workaholic And You Can't Seem To Persuade Him To Take Time Off

Try to create a lot of suspense and anticipation, putting a great deal of time and effort into your *first* getaway. If your spouse has a fantastic time, you'll have less of a problem next time convincing him to take time off work again as he too will look forward to your next encounter.

If your husband is unable to totally isolate himself from his work commitments and ongoing responsibilities, then strike a compromise. Perhaps you can plan a getaway, agreeing to allow him a predetermined amount of time to call his office or attend to his work commitments. During this time, you could have your own free time. Later in the day, you could reconnect for other mutually enjoyable activities.

Remember the Bible gives us admonition to engage in such events.

In Song of Solomon 7:10-12, Solomon's wife says, in effect, "Let's go to the country, find a nice place to stay, spend some quality time together, and make love." (My paraphrase.) Sounds like something I want to budget time for! I'm sure you do too!

❤onclusion

If one of your life's goals is to meet all the needs of your husband and you have chosen to make that a priority, then you will have to proactively arrange your life and schedule accordingly. Noting your realistic, obtainable goals on paper and periodically evaluating your success in achieving them will assist in keeping you focused.

Yes, romantic encounters and sexual play will and should be spontaneous at times, but for the most part you need to give careful attention to *plan* your

Daily **Encounters**

Periodic **Events**

Seasonal **Escapes**

Enjoy!

Life-Changing Questions to Ponder

♥ Have you taken the time to write out your own obituary, noting the important thing(s) you wish to be remembered for?

♥ What are your top three objectives in life?

♥ Do you think planning your life in twelve-week segments would be a viable option for you?

♥ How do you think you can manage your time more effectively? Have you taken the time to evaluate your schedule and identify time- wasters?

♥ When do you and your husband usually arrange for your daily encounters? Your periodic events? Seasonal escapes? Is it time to have a planning meeting with your husband?

♥ Does your husband usually get the 25th hour of your day?

The Life-Changing Word...
Memorize/Meditate

"We should make plans counting on God to direct us."
Proverbs 16:9 (TLB).

♦ ♦ ♦

"Come my lover, let us go to the countryside, let us spend the night in the village ... There I will give you my love."
Song of Solomon 7:11 & 13 (NIV).

My Prayer to the
Life-Changer

Dear God: After reading this chapter, I...

_____

_____

_____

_____

Chapter Eight

How to Make Romance a Part of Every Day

MEETING...

*"There's romance enough at home
without going half a mile for it,
only people never think of it."*
Charles Dickens

Let The Women Speak:

♥ "Who needs romance when you are a senior citizen?"

♥ "After helping kids with homework and taxiing them all over, who has energy for romance?"

♥ "I don't have the money to be romantic – who can afford high-class dining or high-priced entertainment on a regular basis?"

♥ "My husband is a workaholic. He loves to spend all his time at work, I wonder why he doesn't like to come home and spend time with me?"

♥ "My husband says I'm not romantic and he wants me to be creative, but I'm not sure how to do that."

♥ "I'm an overstressed working woman. I don't seem to ever have time to think about this important area except on special occasions, like our anniversary or birthdays."

Practicing Romance - A Part Of Every Day

When I was endeavoring to secure a photo for the front cover of my book, I spent over eight hours viewing hundreds of pictures on the Internet.

While searching under the heading "Couples in Love/Romantic Couples," I found that most photos did not accurately represent my idea of romance.

Most of the photos were of couples walking along a beach, dressed up for an expensive dinner, or on a cruise. While Simon and I have enjoyed some of these most pleasurable outings, to me, they did not represent the kind of romance I can always afford or even want to indulge in on a regular basis.

This led me to consider the question, what is romance?

The dictionary defines romance as "a love story, a love affair, an emotional attraction or aura belonging to an especially heroic era, an adventure or calling..." [1] Somehow this definition didn't quite capture all of my true feelings.

The word "romance" has a multitude of meanings and represents something different to all of us. Quite frankly, it is hard to define specifically because it is not a science or an art. What romance is for one couple, may not be so for another.

As you will have noted, I eventually chose a photo of an ordinary, jean-clad couple who appear to be expressing their love for each other through their smiles, eyes, and hugs.

If we think of romance only in the context of huge, expensive, time-consuming events, we will shortchange ourselves and miss the many daily moments of romance that are all around.

One man expressed it this way:

"Day-to-day life – with careers, children, chores, bills, and all those horribly mundane things that stress and strain – means that a couple has to make a conscious commitment to make romance a part of their lives. My romantic fantasy is not some special place or occasion, such as a remote beach in Hawaii, but to have romance continue as an integral part of our lives, so that time is set aside each day to care for each other. No matter how simple or elaborate, it's not so much the setting but the feeling and attention when we affirm daily, 'You are important to me, I enjoy having you in my life, and I want to take time to celebrate our relationship even if only for a short while each day.' It means never taking each other for granted, and it means always nurturing, caring for each other, and being supportive of each other. It's keeping romance alive in our daily living that matters the most. It's all the little things that constantly remind us that we matter to each other." 2

**Lasting romance exists in a multitude of *small*,
thoughtful, loving actions that are carried out
on a regular basis.
Romance is an attitude
that you can create anywhere, anytime!
One small romantic, thoughtful act can serve as a
catalyst and soon your relationship will be
enhanced.** 3

The secret is to make it a habit. Giving your partner a little TLC every day shows you really care for him and are interested in expressing those feelings to him.

Some women take offense to this idea. They feel that if they have to plan to affirm, or plan romantic gestures, then it is a mechanical project and is not coming from the heart. It doesn't have to be that way. Just as we schedule our time, develop a budget and plan our week's menus, we must also put some time and energy into devising how we can share loving affirmation with our husbands.

If we wait until we "feel" like doing it or only offer spontaneous expressions of our love, the job may not get done and our partner's needs may not be adequately met.

If, on a daily basis, you make your husband feel better than he feels when he is with anyone else, where do you think he'll want to spend his time and attention?

Romance Begins At Home

Kevin Lehman entitled his book *Sex Begins in the Kitchen,* and I would add that *romance* can also begin in the kitchen. If you believe you have to leave your house in order to be romantic, think again. You may be missing some of the greatest opportunities for enhancing your love relationship *right* at home.

"There is romance enough at home without going a half mile for it, only people never think of it" is a true statement. (Charles Dickens)

Consider the following information as you ponder how to enhance your daily romance.

𝓗ow Do You Greet Him?

Whenever you have been away from your mate, even for half an hour, greet him as you come together. When he walks through the door, go to him, give him a hug and a kiss, look into his eyes, and say his name.

In Chapter 5 'How Men Feel,' one man reported, "I love my wife's joy when we meet."

Look genuinely happy to see your spouse – show it on your face, say it in a smile, or write it on a banner or love note. Take your hands out of the kitchen sink and make an effort to genuinely connect.

Try to express a word of commendation or a compliment to your mate in your greeting. For example, "Well, look who's home – my handsome husband!" or "Welcome home, you lovable guy." Try saying, "I'm happy to see the most important man in my life."

If your husband has been away for more than a day, tell him you missed him – don't just think it. If Simon has been away for some reason, I endeavour to be home when he is arriving back. He finds it disappointing if he has been away for a week and he returns home to find an empty house.

"I hate coming home after a long trip to find a note on the counter: 'Gone to a meeting – see you in three hours.' I find this a real letdown," lamented a truck driver.

I recognize it is not always possible to be at home, but it never hurts to make an effort.

"My wife makes these terrific banners and puts them on the front door, on our bedroom door, and in the bathroom. She really goes to a lot of trouble to show me I have been missed, and it makes me feel great! She also asks our children to make pictures and banners that are so meaningful," commented another husband.

Some wives write loving messages in washable marker or lipstick on their bathroom mirror to welcome their mate. One lady at my seminar told me she tapes a loving message on the toilet seat lid as she knows the washroom is the first place he'll head after a long road trip!

If you do not currently greet your partner warmly, start to make it a habit. Make a conscious effort. Who can't afford a few seconds a day to make your husband feel special?

Keep Track Of Your Emotional Responses

To Your Husband

I was challenged to work on this area of my life and began to keep track of my emotional responses to Simon when he came home. I noted my responses for a period of a month.

It was surprising to me how many times I had not stopped to say a kind and warm hello before asking, "Did you remember to pick up the milk?" "Why are you so late for supper?" "Can you go out and pick up the kids?"

On a personal Romantic Reflections calendar, keep track of your mood when your mate arrives home. Are you often irritable? depressed? negative? stressed-out? Or have you been cheerful, positive, and approachable?

While it is impossible to be in a *perfect* mood *at all times* when coping with life's stresses, you can determine to be pleasant most of the time. If you keep track of your mood for a certain time period, you will be able to evaluate if you are a positive, happy person to be around, or more often someone to avoid. (See Romantic Reflections Calendar, page 249.)

One woman who has a full-time job outside the home and is often stressed out has made it a point to arrive home 20 minutes before her husband. During this time, she simply goes and relaxes, enjoying the much-needed peace and quiet. Because she has taken time to do this, she feels she has been able to unwind and is in a better frame of mind when her husband arrives home.

Another working woman plays soft, relaxing music in her car on the way home. By the time she has returned to her home, she has left the day's troubles at work and is semi-relaxed.

This, however, is more difficult for the stay-at-home mother who has had children demanding her attention all day. She can, however, send her children to their rooms for 20 minutes of quiet time before Dad comes home. She then can redirect some of her own energies.

The question we need to ask ourselves is, "Am I a person my husband enjoys and looks forward to meeting, or is he starting to get uptight on the way home, wondering what hassles and havoc will await him upon his arrival?"

How Do You Look?

One day I had been housecleaning most of the afternoon. I was in an old pair of sweats, had no makeup on, and had tousled hair. An older lady who was staying in our home lovingly enquired, "Hey,

Sweetie – are you going to go and comb your hair and put on a fresh coat of lipstick?" She shared how she had made it a habit of "freshening up" before her spouse arrived. She suggested I should consider brushing my teeth, combing my hair, touching up my makeup, and applying a squirt of fresh perfume and in order to look more attractive when my husband came home. She further shared that perhaps my husband had been surrounded by very attractive women all day. "If he continually comes home to the 'bag lady,' he may find it rather disappointing," she chuckled.

I have tried to heed her very thoughtful advice. This simple habit only takes a few minutes. I feel much better about myself and my husband knows I have anticipated his arrival with joy. A career woman could also take a minute to do this before leaving the office to do this as well. She can apply a fresh coat of lipstick and a squirt of perfume, while waiting for the traffic light to turn.

Please note, I am not suggesting that you should greet your spouse every night dressed in an evening gown, or wrapped in SaranWrap™, but I would suggest that you try to look neat, clean, and tidy. If you are in the habit of wearing sloppy clothes, throw some of them out. After attending one of my seminars, one lady went home and promptly threw out the tattered sweats that she continually wore. While that pair of old sweats may be very comfortable and great for gardening, they may not be too appealing to your husband if he comes home to them *every* night.

We need to ask ourselves if the only time we really "dress up" is when we are going out, perhaps for the approval of our other female and male friends.

What Is The Atmosphere Of Your Home?

"After a long, stressful day at work, I can hardly wait to get home; it is like a haven or shelter from the storm. My wife greets me nicely and is happy to see me. I feel I can finally relax. She gives me some space to unwind and most evenings are very pleasant. That is not to say our house is always a picture of perfection. Some days it is chaotic and stressful, but more times than not, our home is my oasis," shared one husband.

In his book, *Men are From Mars, Women are From Venus,* John Gray states that most men need time in their "cave" alone with their thoughts, before they are ready to hear all about your day. Perhaps they have been talking, concentrating, and listening to clients or customers all day and they need to unwind for several minutes. ⁴

I learned this lesson the hard way. During my years as a stay-at-home mom with preschoolers, I eagerly awaited Simon's arrival home and anticipated the opportunity to have some adult conversation. Most often, I had a great deal to share with him and often rifled him with many of questions about his day. Occasionally, I confronted him with the day's crisis (for example, a plugged toilet) before he had a chance to sit down and take off his shoes.

One day, he shared with a touch of exasperation in his voice, "Ruth, will you at least wait until I get my coat off before you start talking to me?" He wasn't trying to be sarcastic; rather, he was just letting me know he needed some space.

Is Your House A Place For Your Husband To "Lay His Head" – A Safe Haven?

While doing research for this book, I tried to locate various examples in the Bible where romantic and sexual encounters had occurred.

One lady who came to mind was Delilah. Although I am not in the least bit impressed by her character, I think there are some things women can learn from Delilah. (Judges 16:4-20)

Most of the sermons I have heard preached about this lady described her as a voluptuous sex goddess who was extremely attractive and sexually appealing. (In actual fact, to my surprise, the Bible does not even make reference to her appearance. Her clothing, makeup or hairstyle are not even mentioned. She is only described as being from the Valley of Sorec.)

So what was it about this woman that made her so attractive and captivated the attention of the mighty man, Samson? Why did Samson continually return to her arms? What was it about this woman that made the Philistine government pay her a huge sum because of what she knew about men? What was it that tempted Samson to keep returning to her bed even when he knew she was trying to find the secret of his strength?

Samson was a powerful, highly driven man, full of purpose. This type of man needs a place where he can lay down his head – a place to unwind and become vulnerable. He needs a haven where he can "take off his armor" and rest for a few minutes or hours.

So what did Delilah know about men? She knew that all men are little boys somewhere deep inside. They are little boys who started their lives by being touched by women. Their mother sang them their first song, gave them their first bath, and when they were tired, they rested their weary heads against their mother's warm breast and fell fast asleep. Most little boys felt safe, protected, vulnerable, and not criticized in their mother's loving arms.

It would appear that that is exactly what Delilah did for Samson. She stroked Samson and talked to him. She listened to him and gave him a place to lay his head.[5] Verse 19 says, *"Having put him to sleep on her lap, she called a man to shave off the seven braids of his hair..."* (NIV). Undoubtedly, she used words to stroke his ego and praised him for his outstanding muscular physique and his handsome face. Her motives were anything but pure and her morals were inexcusable; thus, I am not suggesting that we should use our seductive powers to manipulate our husbands. However, I think her life does illustrate a point.

Is our home a place where our "strong and mighty man" can relax, unwind, trust, and be vulnerable?

Women have no trouble supporting their husbands when they have been defeated. However, we should also allow them to exuberantly share their success.

Many individuals can "weep with those who weep," but they can't "rejoice with those who rejoice." Does your husband know that he can relax and share all his feelings - the good, bad, and ugly - and be assured that they will be acknowledged and accepted?

Often our partners do not want us to help solve their problems, take sides, or comment at all – they merely require an interested person to unload on.

When your husband comes home from "fighting the enemy," will he find a woman who is willing to listen to his heart, his dreams, and his fears? An interesting thought to ponder.

Develop Common Interests

If all that you and your husband do is work, sleep, and eat together, then it is time to cultivate some common interests that you both enjoy.

Perhaps you could join a local team or club, or revive a skill from the past. You could take an enrichment class on a mutually interesting topic or simply enjoy going on a daily walk, run, jog, or bike ride together. Join a fitness club and exercise together. Play games such as chess and dominoes. You can easily take these types of games to the park and play them on a picnic table.

Taking time to develop these common interests can be very relaxing and fun, and it can give you an opportunity to spend many a romantic moment together.

𝒯ouch With Tenderness

Because most men don't readily express their emotions, they often carry stress around in their bodies. They may not realize how tight their shoulders, back, and feet become during the day.

Your partner, like mine, would probably be thrilled to come home to a shoulder rub, a foot rub, or a massage. Massage is wonderful, not only because it relieves your partner's sore muscles and stress from daily cares, but also because it provides an opportunity for him to be in close physical contact with you *without* the pressure to have sex.

Simon and I recently purchased a wonderful hand-held massage unit. Our chiropractor highly recommended it and it has certainly been well-used around our house. Our children even line up for a massage treatment. We call these times "body ministry."

As you will have noted in Chapter 5, many men mentioned the fact that they loved to receive a massage and warm, loving, non-sexual touches from their wives. Perhaps taking a course that teaches how to effectively massage would be something you and your husband might consider.

A study at UCLA found that in order to maintain emotional and physical health, men and women need eight to ten touches a day. Let's ensure our husbands are getting most of their daily quota *from us!* [6]

𝒱alue His Gifts

If your husband has given you jewellery, perfume, or clothing, take good care of these items and wear them often. When you wear them, make a special effort to let him know how much you value them.

Our reaction to the gifts men give us can really encourage them or discourage them from expressing their love in this tangible way in the future.

One friend lamented that she learned this lesson the hard way. Her husband had given her a piece of jewellery that she really didn't like and she thoughtlessly made a sarcastic remark after opening it. She told me, with regret, that her husband has not bought her any jewellery or much of anything since that time. She says she should have just accepted the fact that this gift represented his taste and that he assumed she would like it. "I should have worn it with a smile."

"THEY'RE PERFECT, CHARLES! I'LL THINK OF YOU EVERYTIME I WEAR THEM."

© *Copyright John McPherson (Used by permission)*

Yes, there will be times when our husbands will miss the mark, but we have to remember that they did make *some* effort to please us and we cannot be insensitive to their feelings.

If your husband wants to purchase gifts for you, then give him some *tactful* help. Tell him your preferences and your desired brands and direct him to stores that sell your favorite items. When you are shopping together, take the time to comment on items you appreciate and perhaps he will remember your expressions when the next special event comes up.

When it comes to shopping for clothes, Simon says, "You choose – I'll pay." This works best for us, even when it comes to buying lingerie. "It can be most embarrassing when I buy something that is too big or too small. You go and purchase something that you know will fit and that you like, and I will provide the budget for your expenditures in this area."

He says it makes him feel really special when I purchase something that I know will please him. We're then singing...

"He's happy and I'm happy...

and that's the way it should be!"

Helen tries out her new "Not-Tonight-Honey" nightgown.

© *Copyright John McPherson (Used by permission)*

$\mathscr{P}$lan To Make Mealtime
A Special Romantic Time!

While outstanding culinary skill is *definitely* not my strong suit (just ask Simon), I do feel that I can make mealtime a pleasant, relaxing time by attending to a few rather simple details. Instead of this time being a hassle, a place of conflict and tension, I have tried to ensure that these are pleasant and meaningful occasions.

Since we became parents, our mealtime has become even more creative. At times we have a Backwards Supper (dessert first – this is a favorite). Other ideas include a Green Supper (all food served has to be green), Red Day (everyone has to wear red clothes to the table), various Ethnic Nights (decorations and foods from different countries), etc. We have also eaten our meals in different locations: in the basement, served to each other in bed, in our trailer, and in front of the fireplace. By using these quite simple, yet creative ideas at mealtimes, we, as a couple and as a family, can enjoy affirming, intimate times of fun in the confines of our own four walls.

Quite regularly, we choose to eat our meals by candlelight. Our children also love this atmosphere and lately have been gathering up the candles and lighting them themselves. This simple act creates a special ambience in seconds and at very little cost.

In our home, the TV and radio are banned from the living room and dining room, and are located in another area. We never have to compete with the 6:00 p.m. news, cartoons, or the hockey game over the supper hour or at any other time. Playing soft, instrumental music also helps set a relaxing, restful mood.

Make romance a daily priority.

Be Self-Confident

Men enjoy being with a woman who is comfortable with herself, knows what she thinks and where she is going. Sometimes women are reticent about approaching their mates in a romantic way because they are focusing on their own flaws. "I can't romance him, because I'm not perfect yet." They fear being rejected, looking foolish, or feeling silly.

Remember your mate married you because he was impressed with the unique combination of your mental, physical, emotional, and spiritual attributes. Remember it is much easier to love someone who loves herself.

$\mathcal{K}$eep Up-To-Date On Current Events And On Your Husband's Interests

Showing an interest in your husband's hobbies can be very meaningful to him. If you don't know much about a particular hobby, then perhaps it is time to go to the local library and read up on the subject. The fact that you have made an effort to enter the "world of your husband" may be interpreted as "what is important to me is important to you." Most men find this romantic.

One man who responded to my questionnaire said, "My wife sat down and watched *all* of the hockey finals – she actually seemed interested! It meant a lot to me to have her there."

During my years with preschoolers, I have to admit I lost touch with the outside world. My failure to regularly read the newspaper and watch the news left me with little to discuss with my husband. My world was much too small and I needed to be well-versed on current events to enable me to engage in intelligent, stimulating conversation.

If you know little about your husband's job, ask him to take you on a tour of his plant, meet the office staff, and perhaps read up on his career. By entering his world, you will have a much better understanding of him and how you can best meet his needs when he comes home.

$\mathcal{B}$e Punctual

One man wrote, "*Please*, be on time! Every time I want to take you on a romantic date (ie., dinner or a concert) you are *so* late, it ruins my evening. It makes me feel like time with me is not important."

Enough said. If tardiness is a weakness of yours, this is an area you should seek to improve. Effective daily planning may help or maybe you just need to be satisfied if every strand of hair isn't in its perfect place.

$\mathcal{B}$e Appreciative Of His Compliments

When your husband says, "Wow, you look great in that new dress," don't discredit his compliment. Instead of ignoring it or making fun of it, respond positively. Reply with words such as: "Hey, I'm glad you noticed." "Thanks for your kind words." "You just made my day." "You sure know how to keep your wife smiling!"

Reflect on how you have responded in the past. Perhaps your responses have thwarted or discouraged him from continually affirming you. One man shared, "I try to compliment my wife – she never listens."

Another man said, "My wife needs to think better of herself, she is always putting herself down. She needs to believe I love her just the way she is."

ℭonclusion

In summary, I like what Lucy Sanna says in her book, *How To Romance the Man You Love – The Way He Wants You To*:

"True romance is possible only if it is an integral part of your relationship. It doesn't happen at the snap of a finger. It can't wait for the Caribbean cruise. Rather, it is a steady, practiced way of life. From the moment you greet each other upon waking until you kiss each other goodnight, this way of living requires a romantic attitude, a romantic spirit throughout the day. In today's hectic world, you must make a daily commitment to maintaining romance." [7]

Life-Changing Questions to Ponder

♥ How would you define romance? Is your definition realistic?

♥ How do you usually greet your husband in the morning and/or after work?

♥ How do you dress around the house? Neat? Tidy? Sloppy? Do you need to reassess and improve this area?

♥ What is the atmosphere of your home? Is your house a safe haven most of the time?

♥ Do you touch with tenderness? How could you improve?

♥ Do you value his gifts? When was the last time you showed any appreciation?

♥ Is mealtime at your house usually an enjoyable experience or a battlefield?

♥ Are you up-to-date on your husband's interests and do you show an interest in his work?

♥ Are you appreciative of his compliments?

♥ Are you a punctual person or is this a "bone of contention" in your marriage?

♥ What mutually enjoyed activities should you begin to pursue?

♥ Do you have low self-esteem? How can you work to enhance that?

The Life-Changing Word...
Memorize/Meditate

"A married woman looks for how she can please her husband."
I Corinthians 7:34 – (NIV).

♦ ♦ ♦

"Wash and perfume yourself and put your best clothes on."
Ruth 3:3 – (NIV).

My Prayer to the
Life-Changer

Dear God: After reading this chapter, I...

_____

_____

_____

_____

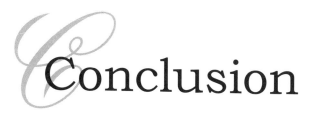

Conclusion

Having just completed this book, you may feel overwhelmed with the amount of data (input) your internal computer has just entered. Your "hard drive" may be full...

Some may ask ... How I can enter, highlight, edit, or delete so much information at once? My suggestion is that you take a methodical, systematic approach. Review and apply *one* chapter at a time. Spend quality time reflecting on all the information shared.

Inch by inch – Life's a cinch...
Yard by yard – Life is hard.

Because the Lord knows the *uniqueness* of your own marital relationship, ask Him to show you what things will apply to your marriage and what suggestions are appropriate for you.

Remember, most change occurs over time and as a result of concerted effort. Don't expect to change everything overnight. Continue to meditate and memorize His Word, as well as pray about ways you can improve your love life.

For others, this book has affirmed what you are already doing and you feel encouraged that you are on the right track.

Whatever your response, the Lord is *most* interested in restoring, refining, enriching, and enhancing your sexual and romantic life. You may not be able to change the person on the other side of the bed, but you can change *you!*

Yes, YOU can be a *sensuous, godly* woman capable of meeting *all* your husband's needs. Remember, *you* are the only one with the *right* and the *responsibility.*

"A blazing fire is not started by piling huge logs on top of one another and striking a match. The way to build a lasting fire is to start small: dry paper, bits of kindling, then small branches and finally logs. The fire must be constantly tended to give warmth and remain bright. In the same way, the fire of your passion is built of small pieces of "kindling." Boughs of love piled on top of one another, thought upon thought, action upon action, until the flame of passion blazes bright. Dear friend, it is worth the effort!" [1]

ℛemember...

Change Your Thoughts

Change Your Life

Delight in this God-given gift of physical intimacy!

"You belong to your lover, and his desire is for YOU!"
Song of Solomon 7:10 (NIV adapted).

May your husband be
"ever exhilarated and captivated with *your* love!"
Proverbs 5:19 (NIV adapted).

Make all your dreams
and romantic fantasies come true!
Enjoy!

ℛuth

The Life-Changing Word...
Memorize/Meditate

Psalm 139:14 – "I am fearfully and wonderfully made, wonderful are your works." (NIV).

(I will choose to love myself and my body. I will accept God's design for me. I will share my sensuous, female body with my husband wholeheartedly.)

Genesis 2:24 – "Therefore shall a man leave his father and mother and shall cleave to his wife and they shall become one flesh." (KJV).

(I will choose to become a separate entity from my parents and be welded inseparably to my husband. I will choose to believe God's command, remembering that He endorses and encourages my meaningful, passionate sexual relationship.)

Philippians 3:13 "Forgetting the past and straining toward what is ahead, I press on..." (NIV adapted).

(I will choose to deal with my past hurts, wounds and sins by confessing them and moving on to enjoy the wonderful life God has planned for me. I will realize my full potential with God's help. I will become the beautiful and whole person He created me to be.)

Song of Solomon 7:10 – "I belong to my lover and his desire is for Me!" (NIV).

(I will choose to believe I am a lovable, valuable, unique woman. I will choose to believe I am the only one with the right and responsibility of meeting my husband's needs.)

Psalms 139:23 – 24 – "Search me, O God and know my heart. Test me and know my anxious thoughts. See if there is any offensive way in me." (NIV).

(I will choose to evaluate my personal thoughts and actions and with God's help will choose to diligently work on any area of weakness in our marriage. I will choose to schedule time with my mate to discuss our ongoing relationship with a willingness to change.)

Song of Solomon 7:11 - "Come, my lover, let us go to the countryside, let us spend the nights in the villages ...there I will give you my love." (NIV).

(I will choose to be a passionate, uninhibited, adventurous lover as described in Scripture and will schedule daily encounters, periodic events and seasonal escapes to enhance and enrich my marriage.)

I Corinthians 7: 3 – 5 – "The wife's body does not belong to her alone, but also to her husband. Do not deprive each other except by mutual consent and for a time so that you can devote yourself to prayer. Then come together again, so that Satan will not tempt you because of your lack of self-control." (NIV).

(I will choose to reserve time and energy for our love life and see it as a priority. I will not use my body as a weapon, tool or bribe or deprive my husband.
I will choose to meet my husband's sexual needs with joy, so I don't expose him to great temptation.)

Song of Solomon 1:2 "Let him kiss me with the kisses of his mouth, for your love is more desirable than gold." (TLB).

(I will choose to accept my husband's endearing expressions of love in various forms. I will choose to accommodate, accept and appreciate his God-given makeup.)

Song of Solomon 5:1 "My lover is radiant and ruddy – outstanding among ten thousand." (NIV).

(I will choose to affirm my husband in every way possible. I will choose to enhance his self-esteem by my words and actions.)

Proverbs 5:19 "A loving doe, a graceful deer, may my breasts satisfy you always. May you ever be captivated by my love." (NIV adapted).

(I will choose to be a creative, ravishing expressive lover. I will choose to put a great deal of effort into fulfilling my husband's expectations and sexual fantasies.)

Song of Solomon 8:7 – "Many waters cannot quench love, rivers cannot wash it away." (NIV).

(I will choose to love my husband through all the seasons of our marriage realizing that adversity and troubles will only draw us closer together and to God. I will choose to continually be adding "kindling" to our "blazing fire of love" and will endeavour to make romance a part of every day ... forever!)

Permission is granted to photocopy pages 300 - 304 for easy and frequent referral.

Remember, only God's Word can transform your mind.

Notes

Before You Begin – Introduction

1 - Bill Hull, *Anxious For Nothing.* (Old Tappan: Revell, 1987), pp. 137-138.

2 - Linda Dillow & Lorraine Pintus, *Intimate Issues.* (Colorado Springs: Random House, 1999), pp. 24-25. (This book addresses 21 questions women ask about sex. It is explicit, informative and tasteful – a must-read for every married woman.)

Chapter One: How God Views Sex

1 - Ed & Gaye Wheat, *Intended for Pleasure.* (Old Tappan: Fleming H. Revell, 1977), p. 16.

2 - Ibid, p. 22.

3 - Ed Wheat & Gloria Okes Perkins, *Love Life For Every Married Couple.* (Grand Rapids: Zondervan Publishing, 1980), p. 26.

4 - Ibid, p. 30.

5 - Ed Wheat & Gloria Okes Perkins, *Love Life For Every Married Couple,* p. 30.

6 - Charles R. Swindoll, *Strike the Original Match.* (Portland: Multanomah Press, 1980), pp. 72-73.

7 - Douglas E. Rosenau, *Celebration of Sex.* (Nashville, Tennessee, 1994), p. 17.

8 - Swindoll, *Strike the Original Match,* pp. 73-75.

9 - Wheat, *Intended for Pleasure.* pp. 22-23.

10 - Linda Dillow and Lorraine Pintus, *Intimate Issues.* pp. 14-16.

11 - Ibid, p. 14.

12 - Ibid, p. 14-15.

Chapter Two: How Your Past Affects Your Present Sexual Life

No endnotes

Chapter Three: How Men Are Wired

1 - Willard F. Harley, Jr. His Needs, Her Needs (Grand Rapids: Fleming H. Revell, 1994), p. 11. (This is an excellent book that will help you and your spouse identify your top five needs.)

2 - John Gray, *Men are from Mars, Women Are From Venus.*(New York: Harper Collins, 1994), p.37.

3 - Linda Dillow and Lorraine Pintus, *Intimate Issues.* p.9.

4 - Willard F. Harley Jr., *His Needs, Her Needs.* (Grand Rapids: Fleming H. Revell, 1994), p.42.

5 - Clifford and Joyce Penner, *Men and Sex.* (Nashville: Thomas Nelson, 1997), p. 21.

6 - John Gray, *Mars and Venus in the Bedroom.* (New York: Harper Collins 1997), p. 139.

7 - David and Claudia Arp, *Love Life For Parents.* (Grand Rapids: Zondervan Publishing House, 1998), p. 130.

8 - Lesley Dorman, "The Three Styles of Sex" *Redbook.* March 1998. p. 93.

9 - Richard Morais, *Porn Goes Public* Forbes online www.forbes.com.

10 - Douglas Rosenau, *A Celebration of Sex.* (Nashville: Thomas Nelson, 1994), p. 188.

11 - John Gray, *Mars and Venus in the Bedroom*, pp. 59-60.

12 - Andrew M. Greeley, *Sexual Intimacy.* (New York: Seabury Press, 1973), p. 86.

13 - Relationships News, *New Woman.* June 1977, p. 77.

14 - Joe Beam, *Becoming One.* (West Montrose: Howard Publishing House, 1999), p. 165.

15 - Dr. Patricia Love and Jo Robinson, *Hot Monogamy.* (New York: Plume, 1995), p. 160.

16 - Editors of *Prevention Magazine* Health Books, "How To Romance the Man" p. 3.

17 - Judith Newman, "How To Be a Sex Goddess In Your Own Home", *Redbook*, October 1996, p. 114.

18 - Pat and Marsha Means, "The High Tech Snare of the Pornographer", *Focus on the Family Magazine*, March 2000, p. 1 of Pastor's Insert.

19 - Willard J. Harley Jr., *His Needs, Her Needs.* (Grand Rapids: Fleming H. Revell, 1994), p. 12.

20 - Willard J. Harley Jr., *His Needs, Her Needs.* (Grand Rapids: Fleming H. Revell, 1994), pp. 43-44.

21 - Janet Wolfe, *What To Do When He Has a Headache.* (New York: Hyperion, 1992), p. 2.

Chapter Four: How the Seasons Of a Marriage Affect Your Sex Life

1 - Norman Wright, *Seasons of a Marriage.* Regal Books, 1982, p. 20.

2 - Clifford and Joyce Penner, *Getting Your Sex Life Off To A Great Start.* (Dallas: Word Publishing, 1994), pp. 28-52 & 112-123.

3 - Sue Johanson, *Sex is Perfectly Natural – but Not Naturally Perfect.* (Toronto: Viking Penguin), p.1.

4 - Bernie Zilbergeld, *New Male Sexuality.* (New York: Bantam,1992), p.65.

5 - Audrey Edwards, "Why 24 Million Women Don't Want Sex" *The Oprah Magazine.* July/August 2000, p. 178.

6 – Ibid, p. 178.

Chapter Five – How Men Feel

No endnotes

Chapter Six – How To Discuss Your Sexual Relationship With Your Mate

1 - Dr. Patricia Love and Jo Robinson, *Hot Monogamy*, pp. 40-41. (Table, stats and quote.)

2 – Ibid, pp. 108-111.

3 – Ibid, pp. 42-65.

4 – Ibid, p. 112.

5 - Linda Dillow and Lorraine Pintus, *Intimate Issues*. p. 18.

Chapter Seven: How To Plan Your Sex Life

1 - Clifford and Joyce Penner, *Men and Sex*. (Nashville: Thomas Nelson, 1997), p. 145.

2 - John Maxwell, "Life, It's Worth Doing", *Injoy Leadership Tapes*.

3 - Tim Elmore, "Living the Life You Were Meant to Live" *Injoy, Serving Today Tapes* Vol. 1. No. 3.

4 - John Maxwell, "Life, It's Worth Doing", *Injoy Leadership Tapes*

5 - Willard F. Harley Jr., *His Needs, Her Needs*. p. 12.

6 - Janet Wolfe, *What To Do When He Has a Headache*. (NewYork: Hyperion, 1992), p. 243.

Chapter Eight: How To Make Romance A Part of Every Day

1 - Webster's New Collegiate Dictionary. (Springfield, MA: Merriam Co., 1977), p. 996.

2 - Lucy Sanna, *How to Romance the Man You Love – The Way He Wants You To*. (Rocklin: Prima, 1996), pp. 131-132.

3 – Ibid, p. 132.

4 - John Gray, *Men are From Mars, Women Are From Venus*. (New York: Harper Collins, 1992), pp. 31-21.

5 - T.D. Jakes, *Woman Thou Art Loosed*. (Shippensburg: Treasure House.1993), pp. 109-111.

6 - Richard Bundschuh and Dave Gilbert, *Romance Rekindled* (Eugene:Harvest House, 1988), p. 64.

7 - Lucy Sanna, *How To Romance the Man You Love – The Way He Wants You To.* p. 142.

Conclusion

1 – Linda Dillow and Lorraine Pintus, *Intimate Issues.* p. 228.

Bibliography

Arp, David and Claudia. *Love Life for Parents, How to Have Kids and a Sex Life Too.* Grand Rapids, Michigan. Zondervan Publishing House, 1998.

Beam, Joe. *Becoming One.* West Montrose, Louisiana. Howard Publishing Co, 1999.

Bundschuh, Richard and Dave Gilbert. *Romance Rekindled.* Eugene, Oregon. Harvest House, 1988.

Dillow, Linda & Pintus, Lorraine. *Intimate Issues.* Colorado Springs, Colorado. Waterbrook Press, 1999.

Dobson, James. *Straight Talk to Men and Their Wives.* Waco, Texas. Word Books, 1980.

Farrel, Bill & Pam, Conway, Jim & Sally. *Pure Pleasure.* Downers Grove, Illinois. Intervarsity Press, 1994.

Ferguson, Dr. David & Teresa and Thurman, Dr. Chris & Holly. *Intimate Encounters.* Nashville, Tennessee. Thomas Nelson Publishers,1994.

Gray, John. *Mars and Venus in the Bedroom.* New York, New York. Harper Collins, 1995.

Gray, John. *Men Are From Mars, Women Are From Venus.* New York, New York. Harper Collins, 1992.

Greeley, Andrew. *Sexual Intimacy.* New York, New York. Seabury Press, 1973.

Harley, Willard, Jr. *His Needs, Her Needs.* Grand Rapids, Michigan. Fleming H. Revell, 1994.

Harley, Willard, Jr. *Love Busters, Overcoming Habits That Destroy Romantic Love.* Grand Rapids, Michigan. Fleming H. Revell, 1992.

Hendricks, Howard & Jeanne. *Husbands and Wives.* Wheaton, Illinois. Victor Books, 1988.

Hull, Bill. *Anxious for Nothing.* Old Tappen, New Jersey. Revell Publishing, 1987.

Jenkins, Jerry. *Hedges, Loving Your Marriage Enough To Protect It.* Brentwood, Tennessee. Wolgemuth & Hyatt, Publishers, Inc.,1989.

Kroeger, Otto & Thusesen, Janet. *16 Ways to Love Your Lover.* New York, New York. Dell Publishing, 1994.

Jakes, T. D. *Woman, Thou Art Loosed!* Shippensburg, Pa. Treasure House, 1999.

Johanson, Sue. *Sex is Perfectly Natural – but not Naturally Perfect.* Toronto, Ontario. Viking Penguin, 1983.

LaHaye, Tim. *Spirit Controlled Temperaments.* LaMesa, California. Living Studies, 1983.

Love, Patricia & Robinson, Jo. *Hot Monogamy.* New York, New York. Plume, 1995.

Maxwell, John. *Your Attitude, Key to Success.* SanBernardino, California. 1984.

Meredith, Don & Sally. *Two Becoming One.* Chicago, Illinois. Moody Press,1999.

McPherson, John. *McPherson's Marriage Album.* New York, New York. Zondervan Publishing House, 1991.

♥♥♥ Undoubtedly, you have thoroughly enjoyed the humorous cartoons throughout this book. I would like to thank John for his permission to use them. I <u>highly</u> recommend buying his great book. ♥♥♥

Nelson, Tommy. *The Book of Romance, What Solomon Says About Love, Sex and Intimacy.* Nashville, Tennessee. Thomas Nelson, 1998.

Parrott, Drs. Les & Leslie. *Relationships 101.* Tulsa, Oklahoma. Honor Books, 1971.

Penner, Dr. Clifford & Joyce. *Getting Your Sex Life Off To a Great Start.* Dallas, Texas. Word Publishing, 1994.

Penner Dr. Clifford & Joyce. *52 Ways to Have Fun, Fantastic Sex.* Nashville, Tennessee. Thomas Nelson, 1994.

Penner, Dr. Clifford & Joyce. *Men & Sex.* Nashville, Tennessee. Thomas Nelson Publishers,1997.

Penner, Dr. Clifford & Joyce. *Sex Facts for the Family.* Dallas, Texas. Word Publishing,1992.

Penner, Dr. Clifford & Joyce. *Restoring the Pleasure*. Dallas, Texas. Word Publishing, 1993.

Penner, Dr. Clifford & Joyce. *The Gift of Sex*. Waco, Texas. Word Publishing, 1981.

Portlock, Rob. *Way Off the Church Wall*. Downers Grove, Illinois. Intervarsity Press,1989.

Rainey, Dennis. *Lonely Husbands, Lonely Wives*. Dallas, Texas. Word Publishing, 1989.

Rosenau, Dr. Douglas. E. *A Celebration of Sex*. Nashville, Tennessee. Thomas Nelson, 1994.

Sanna, Lucy. *How to Romance the Man You Love – The Way He Wants You To*. Rocklin, California. Prima Publishing, 1996.

Smalley, Gary. *For Better or For Best*. Grand Rapids, Michigan. Zondervan Publishing House, 1979.

Smalley, Gary. *Making Love Last Forever*. Dallas, Texas. Word Publishing, 1996.

Swindoll, Charles. *Strike the Original Match*. Minneapolis, Minnesota. Multnomah Press, 1980.

Wheat, Ed. *Love Life for Every Married Couple*. Grand Rapids, Michigan. Zondervan Publishing House, 1980.

Wheat, Ed. *Intended for Pleasure*. Grand Rapids, Michigan. Fleming. H. Revell, 1997.

Wolfe, Janet. *What To Do When He Has A Headache*. New York, New York. Hyperion, 1992.

Wright, H. Norman. *How To Encourage the Man In Your Life*. Dallas, Texas. Word Publishing, 1997.

Wright, H. Norman. *Holding On to Romance*. Ventura, California. Regal Books, 1984.

Wright, H. Norman. *Seasons Of A Marriage*. Ventura, California. Regal Books, 1982.

Young, Ed. *Expressions of Love*. Sisters, Oregon. Multnomah Publishing, 1997.

Zilbergeld, Bernie. *The New Male Sexuality*. New York, New York. Bantam Books, 1992.

Appendix

♥ *Know someone getting married soon?*

♥ *Going to a bridal shower?*

Then Ruth's other book, **Romance 101 ... 101 Creative & Fun Ideas to Keep Your Marriage Alive & Sparking** would make a very practical, thoughtful gift to help the new bride begin and maintain a healthy, growing romantic life. The bride may sincerely desire to meet her husband's needs, but she may lack ideas and/or creativity. **You may also want to purchase one for yourself to pep up your own marriage.**

Order form on next page.

It also makes a ...

♥ Great anniversary gift for daughter or granddaughter!

♥ Great stocking stuffer! Bridal shower gift!

♥ Great tool to enhance any marriage!

Order Information

- ♥ Fax orders: (780) 987-2245
- ♥ Telephone orders: (780) 987-2245
- ♥ On-line orders: www.two-gether.com
- ♥ Ruth's email address: ruthclarence@two-gether.com

Special Note:

Want to share a creative idea for romance?

Send it to the above address ... I'd love to hear from you!

Name: _____

Address: _____

City: _____Prov: _____ Postal Code: _____

Telephone: (   ) _____

(   ) copy (ies) of Two-gether Intimately @ $19.99 $_____

        Add $5.00 per book for postage and handling $_____

(   ) copy (ies) of   Romance 101 @ $9.99 $_____

        Add $3.50 per book for postage and handling $_____

ALL ORDERS MUST BE PREPAID

Total $_____

☐ Visa ☐ Cheque (Cheques payable to Two-gether Ministries)

```
| | | | | | | | | | | | | | | |   | | | |     VISA
```

Visa Card Number   Expiry

Cardholder Signature _____

Ministries

Ruth Clarence

presents one-day seminars entitled:

Two-gether Intimately ...

Understanding & Meeting Your
Husband's Sexual Needs

If you are interested in finding out

how this seminar

could be presented in your area,

Please contact:

Two-gether Ministries ™

780-987-2245

(phone or fax)

Visit website: www.two-gether.com

315